Law and Visual Jurisprudence

Volume 11

The Series Law and Visual Jurisprudence seeks to harness the diverse and innovative work within and across the boundaries of law, jurisprudence, and the visual in various contexts and manifestations. It seeks to bring together a range of diverse and at the same time cumulative research traditions related to these fields to identify fertile avenues for interdisciplinary research.

* * *

In our everyday lives, we experience law as a system of signs. Representations of legality are visually manifested in the materiality of things we see and spatially experience. Methodologically, aesthetic texts of legality semiotically emerge as examples of visual jurisprudence and illustrate the constitutive waltz between social governance, formal law, and materiality.

In its tangled relationship to regulation, the visual complexity of law is semiotically articulated as an ongoing process of meaning imbued with symbolism, memory, and cultural markers. Through a legal semiotics framework of symbolic articulation and analysis, the examination of law that happens in conjunction with the visual expands understandings of how law is crafted and takes root. Additionally, such an inquiry challenges the positivist view of law based within the courtroom as disciplinary spatial practices, the observation of everyday phenomenon, and the visible tethering of regulation to cultural understandings of legality generate a framework of visual jurisprudence. The Series seeks to enliven such frameworks as those in which law happens precisely without formal institutions of law and through which a visual-based methodology of law is crafted through everyday instances of ordinariness that contextualize the relationship between law, culture, and banality.

The Series welcomes proposals – be they edited collections or single-authored monographs – emphasizing the contingency and fluidity of legal concepts, stressing the existence of overlapping, competing and coexisting legal discourses, proposing critical approaches to law and the visual, identifying and discussing issues, proposing solutions to problems, offering analyses in areas such as legal semiotics, jurisprudence, and visual approaches to law.

Keywords: Legal Visual Studies, Popular Culture, Everyday Law, Spatiality, Legal Semiotics, Legal Geography, Legal Materiality, Legal Transplant, Bioethics, Cyber Law, Communication, Heritage and Territory, Design, Marketing, Packaging, Digitalization, Arts.

Olimpia G. Loddo

Intersemiotic Legal Translation

Springer

Olimpia G. Loddo
Department of Law
University of Cagliari
Cagliari, Italy

ISSN 2662-4532 ISSN 2662-4540 (electronic)
Law and Visual Jurisprudence
ISBN 978-3-031-44183-7 ISBN 978-3-031-44184-4 (eBook)
https://doi.org/10.1007/978-3-031-44184-4

This Springer imprint is published by the registered company Springer Nature Switzerland AG
The registered company address is: Gewerbestrasse 11, 6330 Cham, Switzerland

Paper in this product is recyclable.

For Carlo

Preface

The idea of investigating intersemiotic legal translation originated in 2017 when I was working on the research project entitled "The Ontology of Normative Pictures." I developed my research project in a stimulating and resourceful scientific milieu, first in the Department of Law of the University of Cagliari, under the supervision of Prof. Giuseppe Lorini (a pioneer in the study of non-verbal normativity), then as research fellow at the Center for Advanced Studies—South Eastern Europe (CAS SEE). As a fellow at CAS SEE, I had the opportunity to interact with many excellent senior scholars, such as Petar Bojanić and Sanja Bojanić, and with many open-minded colleagues, such as Davide Pala, Monica Cano Abadia, Carlo Burelli, Ivan Cerovac, Natasha Jankovic, Mišo Kapetanović, Gerrit Wagner, and Marko Luka Zubčić. In the same year, I had the opportunity to attend the conference entitled "Cultures in Translation: A Paradigm for Europe" that was organized by the Italian Institute for Culture and the Institute of Philosophy and Social Theory of the University of Belgrade in collaboration with the European Union (EU) Delegation to Serbia, where I presented a paper on the intersemiotic legal translation of normative pictures.

An outcome of that conference was the publication of the first paper on the topic, "Intersemiotic Legal Translation: How to Visualize a Legal Text," which appeared in the collective volume *Cultures in Translation* (Milan-Udine, Mimesis International, 2019) edited by Irena Fiket, Saša Hrnjez, and Davide Scalmani.

Since then, intersemiotic legal translation has been central to my research and has been the subject of some national and international publications. In particular, I published "La traduzione giuridca intersemiotica" in Persio Tincani (ed.), *Diritto e futuro dell'Europa. Contributi per gli workshop del XXXI Congresso della Società Italiana di Filosofia del Diritto Bergamo, 13–15 settembre 2018*, Ornitorinco, 2020, pp. 173–184; "La traduzione giuridica intersemiotica: adattamento versus illustrazione" in *Studi economico giuridici* 2021–2022, ESI, 2021, pp. 449–458; "Intersemiotic Legal Translation: Semiotic Pluralism in Normative Drafting" in *Global Jurist* 22(2022), pp. 537–555; (2022) "Migrazione, traduzione giuridica intersemiotica, Legal design: canali non verbali di comunicazione giuridica finalizzati all'integrazione" in *Annuario ADiM 2021-Raccolta di scritti di diritto dell'immigrazione. Editoriale Scientifica*; "Intersemiotic Translation of Contracts into Digital Environments," with Andrea Addis and Giuseppe Lorini, in *Frontiers in Artificial Intelligence* Technology and Law section, 5(2022), pp. 1–16; "Two Dimensions of the intersemiotic Legal Translation in Digital Environments. Programming legal acts as a resemiotization process," with Andrea Addis, in *2022 31st IEEE International Conference on Robot and Human Interactive Communication (RO-MAN)*, 2022, pp 274–278; and "Traduzione intersemiotica di norme," in *L'ircocervo* 21 (2023), pp. 310–322.

The essays that I published previously on intersemiotic legal translation have certainly contributed to shaping the content of this book. Nevertheless, this book is a distinct and autonomous work and is different from the aforementioned essays. Its purpose is to provide a more extensive and encompassing examination of the subject matter with the aim of presenting a broader perspective.

In 2020, I started writing this book as part of the project "Legal Acts, Images, Institutions: The Form of the Legal Act in the Era of Legal Design" (Department of Law, University of Cagliari). The project Legal Acts, Images, Institutions: The Form of the Legal Act in the Era of Legal Design (Department of Law, University of Cagliari) was supported by Fondazione Sardegna, CUP F72F20000430007.

Within the framework of this project, Giuseppe Lorini (the principal investigator) and Cristiano Cicero (the director of the Department of Law at the University of Cagliari) organized a conference on "Legal Design and Contractual Forms," where I presented a paper on *Intersemiotic Translation of Contracts in the Digital Realm* with Andrea Addis. This conference was also an opportunity to finally meet colleagues with whom I had the pleasure of collaborating during the pandemics in person, such as Anita De Franco and Andrea Addis, and several scholars who inspired my work deeply, such as Raffaele Caterina, Helena Haapio, Patrick Maynard, Polo Moro, Stefano Moroni, and Monica Palmirani.

Intersemiotic legal translation was also a central issue of my talk entitled "The abuse of rights in digital intersemiotic contract drafting" that was given at the SIFD XXXII Congress during the Workshop "Abuse of Law," coordinated and chaired by Silvia Zorzetto. I received several constructive comments both from the chairperson and from the conference attendees.

I am grateful to my colleagues from the University of Cagliari and the Normactivity Research Network who have provided valuable support for my research. I would also like to thank the anonymous referees for their helpful and insightful comments.

Many scholars deserve my gratitude for having contributed directly or indirectly to my scientific growth and to this volume. Among them, I would like to mention Paolo Di Lucia, Francesca De Vecchi, Vincenzo Ferrari, Edoardo Fittipaldi, Lorenzo Passerini Glazel, and Antonio Incampo.

I was deeply inspired by the remarkable contributions to the philosophy of normative language by Amedeo Giovanni Conte, a brilliant philosopher who unfortunately passed away in 2019, his passing was a profound loss to the scientific community.

I am aware that it is impossible to mention all the scholars to whom I am grateful without omitting someone who is important.

However, I cannot avoid mentioning a central figure and a necessary condition for the origin and completion of this research: my mentor Giuseppe Lorini. I had the privilege and fortune to collaborate with him for many years. He inspired, supported, and criticized (always constructively) this book and many other works. I extend my deepest gratitude to him.

Cagliari, Italy Olimpia G. Loddo

Acknowledgment

The book is part of the project *Legal Acts, Images, Institutions: The Form of the Legal Act in the Era of Legal Design* (Department of Law, University of Cagliari) supported by Fondazione Sardegna, CUP F72F20000430007.

Fondazione di Sardegna

Contents

Chapter 1
Introduction

If we were to enter a restaurant in Belgrade, it is likely that we would see ashtrays on most of the tables, except on some of the tables located in a specific area of the restaurant. In this area, we would probably find a sign with an image of a cigarette inside a circle-backslash symbol. If the regulatory statement *забрањено пушење* accompanies the sign, it will not be necessary to speak Serbian to understand that the written part means "no smoking", and that we are not allowed to smoke in that section of the restaurant. According to the Serbian legal system, while it is permissible to smoke in restaurants, every place larger than eighty square meters must have a no-smoking zone in which smoking is prohibited. Thus, the smoking ban in the restaurant is legally binding, and the image of a cigarette in the circle-backslash symbol translates a legally binding verbal norm into a normative picture.

This example does not appear to match the concept of traditional legal translation. The expression 'legal translation' typically refers to translating a verbal legal text in one language into a verbal legal text in another. This widespread understanding is partly due to the overlap of two pan-verbalist (logocentric) traditions, namely the general theory of translation and the general theory of law.

The most widespread concept of translation is expressed well in the words of Umberto Eco, according to whom a translation is "the version from a text A in a verbal language Alpha into a text B in a verbal language Beta."[1]

However, in his studies of translation, Eco himself analyzed a broader vision of translation[2] proposed by another distinguished scholar, the Russian-American linguist Roman Jakobson[3] who, while stating that the interpretation of a sign belonging to one language using a sign belonging to another language was a translation in the "proper sense," coined the term "intersemiotic translation" to describe all those

[1] Eco (2003a), p. 1.

[2] Eco (2003b), p. 372.

[3] Jakobson (1959), p. 233.

O. G. Loddo, *Intersemiotic Legal Translation*, Law and Visual Jurisprudence 11,
https://doi.org/10.1007/978-3-031-44184-4_1

forms of translation that are an interpretation of a sign using another sign that belongs to a different semiotic system.

Translation can be understood as a form of communication. Communication is particularly multimodal in the contemporary era. Words are not the only bearers of meaning, as different types of signs and meaning bearers (such as non-verbal sounds, drawings, pictures, tactile signals, digital artifacts, and material artifacts) play a fundamental role in our social interactions. The concept of translation that Jakobson proposed is able to account for the variety of forms of translation that involve non-verbal sign systems.

In the general theory of law, the idea that verbal language is the basis of legal phenomena is widespread. The idea that identifies legal translation with interlingual translation remains dominant today precisely because of the logocentric representation of law that prevails among jurists.

This logocentric approach does not provide an adequate understanding of the complexity of the law, including its nature, its genesis, and its methods of communication. Using images, diagrams, comics, and illustrations in conjunction with verbal expressions in legal documents, including privacy policies and contracts, is becoming an increasingly common way to communicate legislative innovations and to outline the essential features of current legislation. The use of non-linguistic semiotic systems in legal communication is becoming increasingly common, and is motivated by the need to communicate regulatory messages quickly to an increasingly wide and heterogeneous audience of recipients, many of whom lack specific technical skills and come from different cultural and geopolitical backgrounds.

Apart from words, the non-linguistic semiotic tools that can support the encoding and decoding of messages with legal significance are drawings, material artifacts, and digital artifacts, such as electronic contracts and smart contracts. These legal messages can appear in physical and digital environments, such as web interfaces. Drawings[4], as well as material artifacts and digital[5] artifacts, have already been examined as legal realities and as forms of the manifestation of law.

However, legal theorists have yet to participate in the debate about intersemiotic translation, and intersemiotic legal translation has not been the subject of specific investigations to date. Moreover, no studies have examined the legal drafting and contract drafting techniques using the tools provided by semiology and by general legal translation theory. This volume aims to provide a contribution to fill this theoretical gap.[6]

[4] Porter (2014); Lorini (2019); Lorini and Moroni (2020, 2021).

[5] Katsh (1995); Geer (2007); Brownsword (2019, 2021).

[6] The lack of a specific theoretical investigation does not correspond to an absence of the phenomenon on a practical level. In particular, this book will draw on examples taken from techniques that are actually in use in legal communication. The (more or less) conscious use of intersemiotic translation techniques is gradually spreading among legal practitioners.

In fact, although research focusing explicitly on legal translation has been conducted, there are numerous recent works on intersemiotic translation, and there are legal drafting techniques that a

Thus, this is the first book to provide an analysis of intersemiotic legal translation; that is, those types of legal translation in which the source and the target belong to different semiotic systems: For example, translation from a verbal to a visual semiotic system.

From a methodological point of view, the research integrates studies of intersemiotic translation, which have mainly involved semioticians thus far, with research concerning legal translation, which includes comparative jurists, general theorists of language and translation, and legal theorists.

A three-fold approach was employed in this research. The first approach was the analysis and reconstruction of the conceptual tool of intersemiotic translation. The second approach was a comparison of intersemiotic and legal translations by paying particular attention to the peculiarities of the normative language in general and of legal terms in particular, while the third approach involved the identification of the limitations and the potential that these translation techniques have in legal practice.

The objective of this research, which has a marked multidisciplinary character, is to derive conceptual tools that can be adopted thoughtfully in daily legal practice based on the semiotic and linguistic studies of intersemiotic translation.

The investigation of intersemiotic legal translation has considerable potential from a practical perspective. The intent is not simply to encourage a theoretical reflection on the issue of intersemiotic translation in the legal field, but also to provide professionals and officials who aim to make legal communication more inclusive with concrete tools that will allow them to achieve their objectives more easily.[7]

References

Brownsword R (2019) Law, technology and society: re-imagining the regulatory environment. Routledge, Abingdon

Brownsword R (2021) Law 3.0. Routledge, New York

Eco U (2003a) Mouse or Rat? Translation as negotiation. Phoenix, London

Eco U (2003b) Dire quasi la stessa cosa. Esperienze di traduzione. Bompiani, Milano

Geer D Jr (2007) The physics of digital law. In: Balkin JM et al. (eds) Cybercrime. Digital cops in a networked environment. New York University Press, New York, pp 13–36

Jakobson R (1959) On linguistic aspects of translation. In: Brower RA (ed) On translation. MIT Press, London, pp 232–239

Katsh ME (1995) Law in a digital world. Oxford University Press, New York, NY

semiotician would consider to be forms of intersemiotic translation, no studies have been devoted specifically to intersemiotic legal translation.

[7] This book does not concern the symbolic graphic representation of law, but the intersemiotic translation of the products of the law; specifically, the norms. The works related to the themes of legal iconography are certainly fascinating, but they are far from being the subject of this work, which intends to provide a moment of scientific reflection while focusing on aspects of the life of law that are clearly connected to legal and contract drafting or to the communication of legal norms.

Lorini G (2019) Corporeal drawn norms. An investigation of graphic normativity in the material world of everyday objects. Phenomenology and Mind 17:80–90. https://doi.org/10.13128/pam-8027

Lorini G, Moroni S (2020) How to make norms with drawings: An investigation of normativity beyond the realm of words. Semiotica 2020:55–76. https://doi.org/10.1515/sem-2018-0062

Lorini G, Moroni S (2021) Rule-free regulation exploring regulation without rules and apart from deontic. Journal for the Theory of Social Behaviour:1–15. https://onlinelibrary.wiley.com/doi/10.1111/jtsb.12291

Porter EG (2014) Taking images seriously. Columbia Law Review 114:1687–1782

Chapter 2
What Is Intersemiotic Legal Translation?

2.1 Introduction

Intersemiotic translation is a phenomenon that laypeople frequently encounter in their daily lives. This concept includes translations that serve a normative or a legal purpose, among other examples.

The fact that non-linguistic semiotic entities can have a normative meaning is a condition of possibility for intersemiotic legal translation.

More precisely, signs belonging to different semiotic systems can be used to translate each other if they are capable of expressing similar semantic content and if they can perform similar pragmatic functions. Thus, it is necessary to ask whether non-linguistic semiotic signs can serve as normative signs. The Italian legal philosopher, Giovanni Tarello, proposed that different forms of language could serve various functions, including normative functions:

> For example—according to Tarello—in figurative language, a picture or a statue fulfills the expressive function; a traffic light, an arrow, or an indicator sign fulfills the preceptive function; an illustration, a geographical map, or an anatomical table fulfills the descriptive function [...] Again, for example, in the language of music, a trumpet blast fulfills a preceptive function, the hours struck by a bell fulfill the cognitive function, and a symphony fulfills the expressive function.[1]

Clearly, we can experience non-verbal signs that perform a normative function in our everyday lives.

The concept of intersemiotic legal translation does not manifest itself explicitly in the speeches of theorists, but emerges in practice in the legal sphere whenever a translation involves different semiotic codes.

Legal documents, particularly contracts, are one of the main expressions of contemporary societies, and are often characterized by the need to interact across national and linguistic borders. The use of non-linguistic signs in legal documents is

[1] Tarello (1974), p. 137. My translation.

O. G. Loddo, *Intersemiotic Legal Translation*, Law and Visual Jurisprudence 11,
https://doi.org/10.1007/978-3-031-44184-4_2

increasing rapidly. In the near future, lawyers will often find themselves faced with documents that express legal matters via pictures, graphics, diagrams, and even comics or cartoons.

Due to its specificity, the legal field is strongly divided according to a need for terminological and conceptual rigor and the need to enable people with heterogeneous and sometimes limited technical and linguistic skills to understand legal acts. Based on these premises, some scholars, lawyers, philosophers, and designers have begun to attempt to analyze forms of non-linguistic legal communication that are shared by and are accessible to non-technicians. In doing so, they have spontaneously based their research on non-linguistic semiotic tools that are aimed at clarifying, and sometimes replacing, traditional legal language.[2]

The search for new channels for legal communication and legal production appears to lead to the transposition of legal texts into legal documents characterized by signs from non-linguistic semiotic systems. These forms of transposition that take place in the legal field can be understood as translations precisely because *they are characterized by the total or partial transposition of a source into a target.* [3] More precisely, since they involve different semiotic systems, these legal translations can be traced back to the concept of intersemiotic translation, which is well known to semioticians.

The concept of "intersemiotic legal translation" combines the concept of "legal translation" with the concept of "intersemiotic translation." To investigate its nature, it is, therefore, appropriate to first examine what legal translation means and, subsequently, identify in which terms a legal translation can be considered intersemiotic.

This chapter introduces the concept of intersemiotic legal translation through the tools provided by the studies deriving from the debate on legal translation and those on intersemiotic translation (conducted by semioticians and linguists). The first part provides a brief overview of the theme of legal translation, highlighting the peculiarities connected to the nature of the normative language and legal terms. It focuses on the literature on the topic to develop a comprehensive understanding of "legal translation." Legal translations can be categorized into three types depending on the correlation between the source and the target sign. The *inter-legal translation* (which involves different legal systems) will be distinguished from the *intra-legal translation* (which concerns the same legal system), and the *supra-legal* translation involving supranational entities, such as the EU, that produce legal translations for the different legal systems of the member states. The second part will provide a brief

[2]For the normative use of drawings and artifacts, see Moroni and Lorini (2017), Maynard (2017), Lorini (2019), Aguilera (2019), Loddo (2020), Lorini and Moroni (2020), Lorini et al. (2021), and Dudek (2022).

[3]For convenience, and adopting the lexicon of translation theorists, we will call the object of the translation activity the "source" and the final product of the translator's activity the "target." In this way, it is possible to identify a relationship between a source and a target (or translation) in all types of translations. The way in which the source and the target are connected can vary greatly depending on the translation approach adopted by the translator. These variations are also relevant to intersemiotic legal translations, as will be demonstrated.

account of the evolution of the concept of intersemiotic translation, starting from the distinction introduced in 1959 by Jakobson between intralingual, interlingual, and intersemiotic translation up to the contemporary age, focusing on the relevance that the set of phenomena subsumable under this concept may have for the contemporary jurist. The third part will clarify the concept of intersemiotic legal translation, understood as a species of the genus "legal translation." Finally, a typology of legal translation, including intersemiotic legal translation, will be outlined.

2.2 Defining Legal Translation

When translators translate a legal text, they may have to focus both on strictly linguistic problems and on those deriving from the different legal traditions that come into play in the context of the translation process. The legal system that represents the background of the source text can be different from that of the target legal text. They shall also consider the legal field to which the text refers (such as civil law, criminal law, administrative law, and constitutional law) and, eventually, the different legal systems involved in the translation activity.

Legal translation has long been considered a prerogative of the general translation theories.[4] Translation theorists did not initially consider the peculiarities of legal language, and naively assimilated legal language into other specialized languages (language for special purposes).[5]

2.2.1 Legal Translation as a Translation for Special Purposes

A legal translation is a translation for special purposes. In other words, it is a translation that makes extensive use of technical language; in this case, legal language. As a technical language, legal language must be kept distinct from ordinary language; in fact, many terms that are used in legal language have different meanings in ordinary language. There must surely be some conformity in legal language and ordinary language that would make it possible to attain some degree of clarity in legal documents.[6] However, one must be aware that legal language contains terminology that is much more precise than are the terms that are used in

[4] Šarčević (1997), p. 2.

[5] For a reconstruction of the applications of the various general theories of translation pertaining to legal translation, see Šarčević (1997, 2000).

[6] Lazzaro (1997), p. 205.

ordinary language. In this regard, the Italian legal philosopher Uberto Scarpelli[7] rightly warned lawyers against the "apology for ordinary language."

Reducing legal language to ordinary language is not a suitable way to make legal texts more understandable.

Legal language requires different and complex specialized terminologies, which can vary even within the same legal system depending on the discipline; for example, in the Italian legal system, the concept of possession is understood differently in criminal law and in civil law, while the term *Vernehmung* refers to different concepts in criminal procedure and in civil law in the German legal system.

Legal translation can differ from other forms of translation for special purposes, and therefore uses a specialized lexicon. The difference between legal translation and other forms of specialized translations can easily be observed if one compares the specialized language used by a lawyer to the specialized language used by a physicist, for example.

When translating a scientific term, the translator can refer to a system of concepts that have been developed and homogenized over centuries by an international community of scholars. These scholars are simultaneously the users and the creators of that language. Moreover, the phenomena and objects in that language do not change according to the country or the socio-economic context. For example, Newton's second law expresses the meaning of the term "force": This term can be translated into Catalan (*força*), German (*Kraft*), and Italian (*forza*) without its technical meaning being altered in the translation process.

As is well known, legal terms do not behave in the same way since, when translating a legal-technical term, one often does not find a synonymous term in the target language. For example, the Italian term '*contratto*', the English term 'contract,' and the French term '*contrat*' can refer to legal institutions that are not identical since their characteristics are, at least partly, defined by the different legal systems.[8]

It is crucial to identify the common denominators that unify the names of diverse legal institutions across different legal systems to promote the viability of legal translation. Conversely, it is also crucial to delineate the factors that differentiate these terms, thus rendering interlingual translation a challenging task and intersemiotic translation an even more arduous undertaking.

From this point of view, the theory of legal institutions proposed by the Italian legal philosopher Cesare Goretti seems remarkable. Inspired by Kantian philosophy, Goretti identified *a priori* legal schemes based on the existing relationship between

[7]According to Scarpelli (1995), p. 6 (my translation), "We have actually witnessed, in the philosophy of language [. . .], especially in the British one, to an apology for ordinary language, considered the place of linguistic and mental health. This illusion was soon denied by the universal recognition that the ordinary language is itself the field of multiple 'language-games', generally played without full awareness of the rules of the game. And if it works well in very simple contexts . . . when used in culturally complex areas, it causes an abundance of uncertainties, confusions, and obscurity."

[8]Sacco (2000).

the will and the external world. Goretti presented immutable formal structures, which characterized the condition of the possibility of juridical experiences. At the same time, he highlighted the contingent aspect that characterizes the formation of legal institutions derived from repetitive patterns of actions that cannot arise through a sudden regulatory act by the legislator.[9] Cesare Goretti's institutional theory of law further emphasized the importance of context in understanding legal institutions, which may inform approaches to intersemiotic legal translations.

The relationship between ordinary language and legal language has been the subject of extensive debate. These debates have important implications for intersemiotic legal translation, which requires a thorough understanding of the semantic dimensions and peculiarities of legal language.

The relationship between legal language and everyday language has been a prevalent topic in analytic jurisprudence. In the second half of last century, legal philosophers have recognized the potential for advancement in jurisprudence by studying legal theory through the lens of the philosophy of language.

Legal language certainly has a higher level of precision than does ordinary language, but its *application* may introduce profiles of uncertainty. The uncertainty connected with applying a legal text can affect its intersemiotic translation.

Consider the case that Hart described in *The Concept of Law*, namely "Communication through Example." As we will see, one of the techniques adopted by intersemiotic translators who intend to represent a norm is the presentation of an example of the application of the norm. Thus, the rule "take off your hat when you enter church" can be represented by an image or a cartoon of a man taking off his hat accompanied by a conventional element highlighting its deontic nature. The translation operation thus described raises all the problems highlighted by Hart, such as "How much of the performance must be imitated? Does it matter if the left hand is used instead of the right to remove the hat? Is it done slowly or smartly? That the hat is put under the seat? That it is not replaced on the head inside the church?" [10]

These profiles of uncertainty can, in fact, also be found in visual representations of the same rule, such as the visual representation of a hat inserted in a prohibition sign (Fig. 2.1).

Does the rule only concern white hats, or are black hats included? Does it refer to hats in general, or only to caps? In this case, the task of abstracting the general conduct criterion is also entrusted to the interpreter; in our case, to the recipient of the translation. For this reason, the translator must consider the interpretative skills of the recipient of the text, and eventually combine the two forms of translation by including a linguistic expression such as "no hats" in the target artifact.

For example, an intersemiotic signal representing the prohibition of consuming durian (Fig. 2.2) might not be readily comprehensible to a recipient who is unfamiliar with this particular fruit and its unpleasant odor.

[9] Goretti (1930).

[10] Hart (1961), p. 125.

Fig. 2.1 A sign translating the expression "No wearing hats". From Unsplash. Author rendering

Fig. 2.2 A sign translating the expression "The consumption of durian is not allowed". From Unsplash. Author rendering

The interpretation of this norm may pose a challenge for an individual who lacks knowledge of the regulated behavior; in this case, familiarity with durians and awareness of their strong smell. Conversely, an individual who possesses an understanding of the regulated behavior and perceives the norm as being reasonable will find its interpretation relatively straightforward.

In contrast to the vagueness of the examples, the communication of a general rule via a linguistic expression ("Every man must remove his hat on entering church") appears to be clear, reliable, and definite. The characteristics to be regarded as general guides for behavior are identified through words in this case; they are extracted verbally, and do not remain included with other indicators in a concrete example. To determine what to do on other occasions, a child no longer has to guess what is intended or what will be approved; s/he is not left to speculate about how their behavior must resemble the example in order for it to be correct: S/he has a rule that s/he can apply to him/herself.

However, explicit forms of legal communication often contain "open texture"; they cannot foresee or account for every possible circumstance in which they may apply. As a result, there is room for interpretation and discretion in their application and enforcement.

Conversely, communication by example also helps to fill the gaps and to clarify ambiguities in explicit rules, and provides a more nuanced understanding of social practices.[11]

2.2.2 Interlegal Translation, Intralegal Translation, and Supralegal Translation

Legal translation does not operate solely on the linguistic level, as it also involves a legal system. In this sense, terms referring to legal concepts and legal institutions express the distinctive features of a particular legal system.[12]

Legal vocabulary varies according to the legal system that produces it.[13] The absence of a precise correspondence between legal terms in different languages, often highlighted by comparative jurists, poses an important obstacle to legal translation.[14]

However, the language adopted by the translator must be kept distinct from the legal system to which it refers.

Two different states can adopt the same official language and be governed by different legal systems. In this case, a lack of synonymy can also arise in the context of the same natural language. For example, Italian and French are the official languages of Italy and France. In addition, they are both official languages of

[11] Intersemiotic legal translators must take the aforementioned aspects into consideration, together with other relevant factors in order to perform their tasks effectively. For example, Ronald Dworkin (1988) proposed that the evaluative character of legal language, with its semantic and moral dimensions, differentiated it from everyday language. This also has implications for intersemiotic legal translations, which may require an understanding of the historical, cultural, and ethical background of both the source and the target artifacts. This includes several axiological considerations that can affect the interpretation of the translation output.

[12] Legal concepts have been the subject of discussion among philosophers and legal theorists for an extended period. For a reconstruction of the analytical theory of legal concepts in the last century, see Pintore (1990). The general theory of legal concepts has been the subject of an edited collection by Hage and von der Pfordten (2009). For legal concepts, also see the more recent work by Bajčić (2017).

[13] Lauzière (1979).

[14] Mac Aodha (2014).

Switzerland. However, as Rodolfo Sacco[15] pointed out, '*possesso*' and 'possession' in France and Italy indicate the *de facto* power over something exercised via *animus domini*[16]; the same term in Swiss law does not imply that possession requires the *animus domini* in any way.

According to Umberto Eco,

> [w]e decide how to translate, not on the basis of the dictionary, but of the whole history of two literary cultures.[17]

Similarly, a translator who translates a text into a language other than that adopted in the legal system undergirding the source text must consider two different legal cultures, bearing in mind that the terms in the source text refer to the legal institutions based on the norms established within a particular legal system.

A translation that implies the passage from one legal system to another is an *interlegal translation*.[18] This form of legal translation is particularly frequent in comparative studies.

However, legal translation can also take place within the same legal system. For example, consider the legal systems that promulgate laws in several official languages. An example is all those national legal systems (such as Canada and Switzerland) that promulgate their legal norms in two or more official languages. In these cases, the translation process is an integral part of the legislative procedure. For the sake of clarity, we could call this type of translation an *intralegal translation*.

The third type of legal translation is *supralegal translation*, which involves supranational entities such as the EU. In this case, the products of the translation are addressed to all of the national legal systems of the countries that have joined the supranational organization.

2.2.3 Isofunctional Legal Translation Versus Heterofunctional Legal Translation

Literal translation is the earliest known legal translation technique; it involves translating a legal text word for word from the source text to the target text. For a long time, it was believed that the only goal of a translation was the syntactic correspondence between the source text and the target text; that is, each syntactic unit of the source text should correspond to an analogous unit in the target text. Because different languages have different syntactic rules, this technique is outdated

---

[15] Sacco (1994).

[16] The expression *animus possidendi* refers to the intention to exercise a right in rem over a specific item (for example, as an owner or usufructuary).

[17] Eco (2001), p. 13.

[18] Cao (2007), p. 23.

and can cause errors and inaccuracies. It also fails to account for idiomatic expressions and may neglect important semantic nuances.

However, jurists and theorists of normative language continued to believe widely in the importance of maintaining close adherence to the original text in the process of translation; this adherence did not only concern individual words, but also entire phrases or expressions. In fact, the focus is on translating semantic units rather than on translating literally (word for word).

For example, according to Tarello:

> Translating means [. . .] replacing an expression (of a verbal language [*lingua*], or another type of semiotic code [*linguaggio*]) with another expression (of the same or another language, of the same or another semiotic code) equivalent to the first; that is, capable of producing the same communication [*la stessa comunicazione*] that is produced by the first.[19]

Tarello highlighted that, in a translation, the source text and the target text are equivalent because they convey the "same communication." Similarly, with specific regard to legal translation, the Polish legal theorist Jerzy Wróblewski wrote:

> The legal translation aims at the equivalence between linguistic expressions [. . .] formulated in a language linked to law.[20]

The idea of a legal translation as an equivalence between linguistic expressions is largely hindered by the *anisomorphism of languages*; that is, the absence of one-to-one equivalence between elements in different languages. Some legal terms may be untranslatable because no term in the target language corresponds to the legal institution mentioned in the source text. In other cases, there may only be partial equivalence.[21]

The situation is even more complex in the case of intersemiotic translations. Different semiotic systems can be subjected to different constraints concerning not only the lexicon, but also the syntaxis.

For example, syntactic rules regulating the spatial position of the graphic signs in a normative picture differ from the syntactic rules that regulate the order of the words in a text.[22] In other words, each semiotic system is governed by its own syntactical rules. [23] For example, the syntax of normative pictures can be analyzed in terms of forming signifying units that combine icons or conventional signs.[24] Moreover, the

---

[19]Tarello (1974), p. 138.

[20]Wróblewski (1986).

[21]Mac Aodha (2014), p. 219.

[22]Studnicki (1970); Wagner (2006). Some constraints regulate the use of statements. These constraints are part of the set of rules that regulate linguistic practice. Similarly, there are constraints in pictorial practice. These constraints are less complicated than are linguistic ones. Therefore, on one hand, they can be learned easily; on the other hand, they can only be used in a limited set of situations.

[23]Tijus et al. (2007), p. 23.

[24]Mounin (1970), p. 157.

syntax of normative artifacts regulates the spatial location[25] and their capacity to compose illocutionary sequences in the framework of specific semiotic systems.[26]

However, these obstacles can be overcome by deviating from the literal translation and interpreting the source text with the assistance of the resources provided by judicial decisions and doctrine.[27]

More recently, the idea that translation cannot be considered a mechanical process of transcoding based on the search for equivalents has become dominant among translation scholars.

For example, according to purpose-oriented translation theories, the expressions that constitute the target text do not need to match those of the source text precisely. According to Hans Vermeer:

> Any transfer of simple elements [. . .] misses the point. A faithful translation of a source text can lead to an 'unfaithful' target text.[28]

According to Vermeer, the translated text must perform the same function and produce the same effects as the source text.

The theorist of legal translation, Susan Šarčević,[29] adopted the functionalist concept of translation and applied it to legal translation, proposing a redefinition of legal translation in a pragmatic sense since, according to her, a legal translation should be viewed as a communicative act with a specific purpose. Šarčević denied that a legal translation could be reduced to a transcoding operation.[30] According to Šarčević, a legal translation must not be assessed in terms of formal correspondence between the source text and the target text, as its ability to produce equivalent legal effects should be considered. In particular, Šarčević referred to the interpretation and application by the courts referring to legal texts that have been translated into different languages.[31] In other words, Šarčević argued that legal translation was not a simple mechanical process of transcoding the words and structures in the source text into the target language, but was rather a complex activity that required consideration of the communicative purpose and legal context of the text. Šarčević mainly focused her analysis on "authenticated translations of legal instruments having the force of law."[32] In this sense, a translation of a (valid) legal text is faithful if it is able to produce the same legal effects as the source text within the legal system in which it is applied.

---

[25] Scollon and Scollon (2003), p. 157.

[26] Studnicki (1970), p. 149.

[27] Mac Aodha (2014), p. 219.

[28] Vermeer (1998).

[29] Šarčević (1997), p. 71.

[30] Ibid., p. 55.

[31] The theory of legal translation supported by Šarčević is strongly influenced by the *skopos* theory. See Vermeer (1978); Nord (1997).

[32] Šarčević (1997), p. 277.

However, we can speak of legal translation even if a translated text does not have the same function as the source text.

In other words, the text of a legal norm that imposes a sanction as a consequence of certain conduct can be translated into English for the use of tourists, but the translation has a purely descriptive function, even if it concerns a norm; it certainly does not have the same legal function as the source text.[33]

In this regard, we can differentiate an *isofunctional translation* from a *heterofunctional translation*.

An isofunctional translation occurs when the source text has the same function as the target text; for example, translating a European regulation into the twenty-four official languages of the EU.[34]

By contrast, the translated text does not fulfill the same function as the source text in heterofunctional translations. An example of a heterofunctional legal translation is the translation of a legislative text by a comparatist: While the legislative text has a predominantly normative function, the translation performed by a scholar of comparative law has a predominantly descriptive function. Therefore, it is necessary to differentiate the function of legal terms within the target text (which, for example, in a text of comparative law, have the function of describing norms) from the function of the legal concepts in the legal system to which they refer.

Legal translation implies considering legal issues in the context of both isofunctional and heterofunctional translations.[35] The legal system assigns specific technical meanings to certain terms in ordinary language. Moreover, since legal systems are dynamic, they can introduce new terms (for example, by establishing them autonomously or importing them from emerging social practices or other legal systems) or provide new interpretations of old terms.

The functionalist conception of translation highlights only one of the possible relationships that link the source text to the target text, namely the teleological relation; that is, both texts share the same *τέλος*.[36]

The functionalist conception of translation placed the function of the target text at the center of the theoretical investigation. This function (whether or not it is identical to the source text) plays a fundamental role in the translator's stylistic, semiotic, and lexical choices.

It should be pointed out that there is a difference between the function of the act of translation and the function of the product of translation. The act of translating certainly has the function of creating a new text that has a relationship with the source text. However, the nature of this relationship can vary, and the source text and

---

[33] Harvey (2004).

[34] The identity of the functions of the source text and the target text makes interpretation particularly problematic in the legal field if discordant translations are produced. Lastly, see the controversy caused by the Italian translation of European regulation no. 935/2021.

[35] However, we can consider the target text and the source text legal texts if they derive their meaning from a state or supra-state legal order, or from the juridical experience acquired in the common civil conscience.

[36] For the relationship between the nature of an act and the function thereof, see Incampo (1997).

the target text can also have different functions. Translation can be understood in terms of two distinct aspects, namely purpose (teleology) and nature (morphology).

The purpose of translation refers to the intended outcome or effect that the translation aims to achieve; that is, the goal or objective of the translation process. The nature of translation is related to the inherent characteristics and qualities of the act or content being translated.

Accordingly, we could distinguish between *heterofunctional translation* and *isofunctional translation* (which focus on the effects) and *isomorphic translation* and *heteromorphic translation* (which focus on the type of communicative act that is translated, such as a description or a prescription). Based on this distinction, we can create a taxonomy of four types of translations:

(i) Isomorphic heterofunctional,
(ii) isomorphic isofunctional,
(iii) heteromorphic isofunctional, and
(iv) heteromorphic heterofunctional.[37]

Isomorphic isofunctional translations. In this case, the source text and target text have the same function, and the aim of the translation is to produce the same effect as the original text. However, the nature of the translated act remains the same in both the source and target texts. For example, the translated text of a European regulation in the twenty-four official languages of the EU is an isomorphic isofunctional translation because it maintains the same legal status and aims to produce the same legal effects.

Isomorphic heterofunctional translation. The source text and target text have the same nature, but the translation aims to produce a different effect from that of the original text. For example, the translation of an old contract to create a new agreement while modifying some clauses in the target text is an isomorphic heterofunctional translation.

Heteromorphic isofunctional translation. The source text and the target text are different kinds of acts, but the purpose of the translation is to produce the same effect as the source text. An example could be translating a legal document that prescribes certain actions as a description of that document that is aimed at providing normative information addressed to a specific audience.

Heteromorphic heterofunctional translation. This type of translation refers to a translation in which both the nature of the act being translated and the intended effect of the translation are different from the source text. For example, the description of a law in the context of a campaign to promote a referendum aimed at abolishing that law has is heterofunctional and heteromorphic in nature. The target text has a

[37] Vermeer considered the teleological concepts of aim, purpose, intention, and function to be equivalent, subsuming them under the generic concept of skopos. Nord proposed a more articulated distinction among *aim*, *purpose*, *function*, and *intention*. He called the function the meaning of the text from the receiver's point of view and the aim and the purpose the final and the provisional results; the intention is the plan of action concerning both sender and receiver. See Nord (1997), p. 28.

Table 2.1 In this scheme, the rows represent the nature of the act being translated, and the columns represent the purpose of the translation. The four quadrants of the table represent the four types of translations

Nature of the act being translated	Purpose of translation	
	Isofunctional	Heterofunctional
Isomorphic	Isomorphic isofunctional translation	Heteromorphic isofunctional translation
Heteromorphic	Heteromorphic heterofunctional translation	Heteromorphic heterofunctional translation

different nature from the source text and, at the same time, does not aim to condition the behavior in the way indicated by law but to mobilize voters to bring about the abrogation of the described law. In other words, the campaign's portrayal of the law, in its effort to encourage a referendum for its abolition, demonstrates a distinct contrast in both function and form. The campaign text diverges from the original legal text and does not aim to influence behavior in accordance with the law. Instead, its primary objective is to mobilize voters and to gain support to revoke the law in question (Table 2.1).

2.3 Defining Intersemiotic Translation

2.3.1 Three Types of Translation According to Roman Jakobson

According to Jakobson, translation is the interpretation of a sign via another sign that has the same meaning.

Jakobson adopted this definition of translation in his paper *On Linguistic Aspects of Translation*, which is well known among linguists, semioticians, and translation theorists for introducing the concept of "intersemiotic translation." In the paper, Jakobson differentiated among three different types of translation:

1. *Intralingual* (translation or rewording);
2. *interlingual* (translation or translation proper); and
3. *intersemiotic* (translation or transmutation).[38]

Intralingual translation is defined as the interpretation of a verbal sign by means of other signs in the same language. This type of translation can consist of using a synonymous term or a circumlocution.[39]

[38] Jakobson (1959). Reissued in Jakobson (1971a), pp. 260–266.

[39] The impossibility of producing a translation that is the exact equivalent of the translated text can be observed in intralinguistic translations. A synonymous term is never a perfect equivalent, even within the same language; for example, according to Jakobson, "every celibate is a bachelor, but not

By contrast, *interlingual translation* is defined as the interpretation of a verbal sign using another verbal sign that belongs to a different language. Finally, a translation may involve different semiotic codes: This is the case with Jakobson's third type of translation, namely *intersemiotic translation* or transmutation.

Intersemiotic translation is based on "intersemiotic relations" that connect different semiotic codes; as Jakobson pointed out:

> We find [. . .] various types of intersemiotic relations, such as the transition from gestures to words, from words to gestures, from words to pictures, etc.[40]

Clearly, this triadic division has been the subject of criticism by semioticians who have proposed alternative classifications. For example, Torop's[41] translation theory also started from Jakobson's tripartition and differentiated among textual, metatextual, intextual, intertextual, and extratextual translations. Umberto Eco (2001) proposed an alternative classification that also took translations from verbal signs to behaviors into consideration.[42]

More precisely, Eco differentiated among *interpretation by transcription*, *intrasystemic interpretation*, and *intersystemic interpretation.*

Interpretation by transcription relies on automatic substitution; it does not involve any interpretive decisions, and does not take the context or circumstances of the original statement into account. A good example of this is the substitution of Morse code for the code (letters) of the alphabet.

In Eco's view, *intrasystemic interpretation* may occur within the same natural language or within other semiotic systems. The former encompasses various methods of interpreting natural language through the language itself, such as synonymy, definitions, paraphrasing, inference, commenting, and even parody. The latter takes place within non-linguistic semiotic systems; an example of this would be when a musical composition is transposed into a different key. Performance is an important subfield of this form of interpretation; in the case of performance, interpretation can be expressed through various mediums, such as the execution of a musical composition, the choreography of a ballet, or the presentation of a theatrical play.

Intersystemic interpretation implies significant variations in the substance of the expression, and intersystemic interpretations can occur among different linguistic systems. The most obvious case is precisely that which Jakobson called translation proper, or interlinguistic translation. Intersystemic interpretation can also occur among non-linguistic systems, which Jakobson called intersemiotic translation. Important subfields of this form of interpretation are "parasinonimies" and "adaptations." In parasinonimy, an object is displayed to facilitate the understanding of

---

every bachelor is a celibate." In legal language, which is a technical language, this type of translation poses even greater problems than it does in ordinary language, as seemingly synonymous terms can indicate completely different legal institutions.

40 Jakobson (1971b), p. 330.

41 Torop (2000).

42 Eco (2001).

verbal expressions. In art studies, adaptation refers to transforming one artistic work into another; this can include adaptations of literature in cinematographic mode. Adaptation is considered to be a form of intersemiotic translation because it involves the transfer of meaning from one semiotic system to another. For example, with regard to movie adaptations of literary works, literature uses words, while movies combine moving images, sounds, and dialogue to communicate meaning.

Semioticians have conducted studies of translation to illuminate various phenomena, but most of the phenomena they have considered relate to art studies or commercials. There is no doubt that the fact that they have focused on non-legal studies has affected their analyses.

The translations of artistic expressions into different semiotic systems are indeed more intricate and nuanced than are those that occur within the legal realm. As the legal order is indisputably permeated by various elements emanating from the cultural context, there are definitely some echoes of them in legal practice.

For example, Norberto Bobbio stated that the language used by a lawyer during a closing argument included an expressive function in addition to the normative function, namely that of arousing certain emotions.[43] The career routes of lawyers and actors differ significantly, as they have contrasting technical skills and diverse backgrounds. Although there may be similarities in their communication techniques, comparing a lawyer's speech to an actor's performance would be inaccurate and misleading because their goals and priorities are different. Therefore, we could not include what Eco called "performance" in the form of intersystemic interpretation except at the price of gross forcing, which would risk making us lose sight of what we should clarify instead; that is, the specific characteristics of legal experience.

The present reconstruction of the phenomenon of intersemiotic translation in the legal field takes the different typologies of translation elaborated by semiologists into account. However, since we are considering concepts that were created and applied specifically to phenomena that are linked to non-legal spheres, the classification proposed by Jakobson, although extremely generic compared to the subsequent ones, is preferable for our purposes. In addition to its generality, it is both clearer and more flexible.[44]

It is important to point out that intersemiotic translation can occur within the same discourse, or we can speak of semiotic translation even in cases of *intersemiotic redundancy*. In this case, the same meaning is expressed several times in the same speech (for example, in the same document) via signs belonging to different codes.

Of interest, in *On Linguistic Aspects of Translation,* the definition that Jakobson proposed highlighted a passage from words to signs belonging to other semiotic codes; for example, from verbal art into music, dance, cinema, or painting. According to Jakobson, an intersemiotic translation is

> an interpretation of verbal signs by means of signs of non-verbal sign systems.[45]

[43] Bobbio (1993), p. 54.

[44] For a reconstruction of Jakobson's tripartite debate, see Jia (2017).

[45] Jakobson (1971a), p. 261.

However, the concept of intersemiotic translations also appears to include the translation from a non-verbal system to a different non-verbal system. In this sense, Jakobson discussed an "intersemiotic transposition from one system of signs into another."[46]

The essential element of transmutation is the *interpretation of a sign belonging to a semiotic system into another sign belonging to a different semiotic system*. In fact, in the essay *Aphasia as a Linguistic Topic*, Jakobson adopted this wider definition and stated that transmutation was characterized by the "transposition from one sign system to another"; according to Jakobson, examples of intersemiotic translation included the indication of an image or an object to recall the name of that object in the recipient's mind.[47]

More recent studies of intersemiotic translation appear to have endorsed this wider concept whereby the translation from words to other types of signs is only one of the possible examples of intersemiotic translation. As Queiroz and Aguiar[48] pointed out, the term became broader, and now designates relationships between systems that are different in kind; it is not restricted to the interpretation of verbal signs.[49] Therefore, translation can involve different semiotic systems, and none of the systems involved may be verbal.[50]

According to the semiotician Nicola Dusi, the link between the source and the target text is an essential aspect of translation. Dusi underlined that this link did not necessarily consist of an exact correspondence. According to Dusi, an intersemiotic translation is a representation of a source text in one or more semiotic systems. Despite the fact that an intersemiotic translation does not include all aspects of the source text, because perfect semantic equivalence is not required, the content of the target text should relate to the content of the source text in some way.[51]

2.3.2 Intersemiotic Legal Translation as a Tool for Legal Drafting

As mentioned previously, intersemiotic legal translation refers to all the forms of legal translation that use at least two different semiotic codes.

For the purposes of this study, we considered both translations that produced legally binding documents and translations that produced non-binding documents. Accordingly, a legal translation must be viewed as any form of transposition based on a legal document (see Sect. 2.2.3) Examples of intersemiotic legal translations in

[46] Ibid., p. 269.

[47] Jakobson (1971c), p. 235.

[48] Queiroz and Aguiar (2015).

[49] *Vide* Plaza (1987); Gorlée (2004).

[50] Dusi (2015), p. 182.

[51] Ibid., p. 184.

this sense include graphs and diagrams illustrating parts of legal documents, comic-book adaptations of contractual texts, animations or videos that express the content of legal texts (for example, to communicate the introduction of new legislation to a particular area of a company), and safety signs that are characterized by normative images that illustrate the norms that were originally expressed verbally. Furthermore, forms of legal translation include those that occur within the same legal document. Hence, the illustrations in the *Sachsenspiegel*[52] (see Sect. 5.2.2) can be considered to be intersemiotic legal translations.

Intersemiotic translation is a crucial component of several strategies of normative drafting that fall under the umbrella of legal design, which refers to the application of human-centered design techniques to normative drafting.[53]

Specifically, the legal design techniques applied to legal drafting, contract drafting, and institutional communication make (more or less consciously) extensive use of this form of translation.

Human-centered design is a design approach that identifies one or more types of people as the main users of an artifact and places their physical, psychological, and cultural characteristics at the center of the design.[54] In this sense, legal design is a (heterogeneous) set of techniques for designing and drafting (paper and digital) legal documents that are gradually achieving success among jurists and legal practitioners. These normative drafting techniques aim to facilitate and simplify legal communication to make it accessible to the user; that is, the contractor or layperson who needs to understand the content of the legal document.[55]

Among the strategies adopted to improve the accessibility of legal documents and to facilitate understanding of the regulatory message is the recurrent use of non-linguistic semiotic codes that are selected based on the recipient's skills. Accordingly, intersemiotic legal translation is a fundamental strategy for legal designers.

---

[52] The *Sachsenspiegel* is one of the oldest surviving legal codes in the German language. It was written in the early thirteenth century in the Saxon region of Germany, and is named after this region. It was compiled by the Saxon nobleman Eike von Repgow, who based it on older legal codes and customary law. The text covers a wide range of legal topics, including property law, inheritance law, family law, criminal law, and procedural law. The manuscript is decorated with a series of miniatures, or small illustrations that serve as visual aids to the text. They were created by several different artists, and depict scenes related to the legal content of the text, such as the transfer of property, the settlement of disputes, and the administration of justice.

[53] Hagan (2018).

[54] Human-centred design is a design process that is based on psychological characteristics and the human capacity for perception. For more about this subject, see Giacomin (2015).

[55] Haapio and Passera (2021), Haapio and Hagan (2016), Berger-Walliser et al. (2017), Haapio et al. (2020), and Brunschwig (2021).

2.3.3 *Intersemiotic Legal Translation in a Typology of Legal Translation*

The concept of intersemiotic legal translation can be considered to be a species of the genus "legal translation." Applying Jakobson's tripartition to the legal sphere can help to clarify the distinction between the semiotic and the legal dimensions of legal translations. The topic of intersemiotic legal translation meets (but does not overlap with) the theme of legal translation. The investigations of legal translation[56] focus on interlingual translation, and tend to overlap with the semiotic code and the deontic code,[57] the system of signs and the system of norms. It is easy to confuse the two levels since it is precisely the deontic code that gives a specific deontic meaning to the terms in the semiotic code. Legal translation involves more than simply translating deontic words, which are words that express obligation, permission, or prohibition. Legal translation also requires an in-depth understanding of the terminology used in both the source and in the target legal systems. Legal terms often have specific meanings that are not always clear based on their literal translations, and legal translators need to be able to convey these meanings accurately in the target language. In addition, legal translation often involves technical and specialized vocabulary, such as scientific or financial terms. Legal translators must be familiar with these specialized terms and be able to translate them accurately into the target language.

The term "code" is obviously evocative for lawyers, legal historians, and legal theorists. It is possible to analyze a legal code in semiotic terms, as some semioticians[58] have done for the highway code. However, this does not mean that a legal code is a semiotic code.

Legal codes contribute to constructing one of the possible semantic and pragmatic dimensions of a semiotic code; they are not unrelated to the semiotic code, but do not coincide with it. Legal codes are constructed and interpreted within a specific cultural and linguistic context. The meaning of legal codes is not inherent in the words themselves, but is shaped by the social and cultural practices of the society in which the codes are used. Legal codes rely on language and other signs to communicate meaning, but they are constructed and interpreted within a larger cultural and linguistic context.[59]

---

[56] See, for example, Rotman (1995), Šarčević (1997), Alcaraz Varó and Hughes (2002), Cao (2013), Cheng et al. (2014), and Mac Aodha (2014).

[57] The term "deontic code" appears in the essay *Codici deontici* (*Deontic codes*) by Amedeo Giovanni Conte (1976). An example of a deontic code is a traffic code. Despite not being irrelated, it is possible to draw a distinction between a traffic code (as a deontic code) and a system of traffic signs (as a semiotic code).

[58] For the semiotic and deontic aspects of traffic signs, see Studnicki (1970), Mounin (1970), Wagner (2006), Maynard (2017), and Dudek (2022).

[59] Ricca (2023).

This reflection on the term 'code' is relevant for this investigation of intersemiotic legal translation because it allows us to place the intersemiotic legal translation within a typology that is more articulate and more relevant from a legal point of view than is the one that Jakobson proposed (see Sect. 2.3.1).

Let us imagine a French-speaking jurist with a semantic background based on the French Civil Code and, more generally, on the French legal system. Nothing prevents this French jurist from using his or her mother tongue to write an essay in which s/he analyzes the peculiarities of Belgian contract law by comparing it to French contract law. Using the classification proposed by Jakobson, we could speak of an intralinguistic translation in this case, since the jurist would use the French language to write his or her essay and would examine the norms expressed in French. However, this would be an interlegal translation because it would involve two different legal codes, namely French law and Belgian law.

Therefore, we can insert the intersemiotic legal translation into a typology constructed via a combination of the tripartition proposed by Jakobson Sect. 2.3.1), which mainly refers to the semiotic dimension, and the distinctions among intralegal translations, interlegal translations, and supralegal translations, which concern the legal code instead (Sect. 2.2.2).[60] Thus, we can identify nine different types of legal translations: (i) intralegal intralingual translations, (ii) interlegal intralingual translations, (iii) supralegal intralingual translations, (iv) intralegal interlingual translations, (v) interlegal interlingual translations, (vi) supralegal interlingual translations, (vii) intralegal intersemiotic translations, (viii) interlegal intersemiotic translations, and (ix) supralegal intersemiotic translations.

1. *Intralegal intralingual translation.* We can speak of intralegal intralingual translation if a paraphrase is used to clarify the meaning of a legal document within the same legal system.
2. *Interlegal intralingual translation.* An intralingual interlegal translation involves two legal systems that share an official language. For example, French is the official language in both France and Canada; in this case, the target text refers to a legal system but is intended for an audience that, while speaking the same language, is governed by a different legal system.
3. *Supralegal intralingual translation.* The legal texts of supranational legal systems may be the subject of explanatory notes, which clarify supranational regulations and the criteria for their interpretation. These explanatory notes make extensive use of intralinguistic legal translations. As they are paraphrases, they are presented in the same language as the source text, and have the aim of clarifying the institutions in a particular supranational legal order.
4. *Intralegal interlingual translation.* An intralegal interlingual translation is an interlingual translation within the same legal system. For example, an intralegal interlingual translation is the basis of the promulgation of a law in a legal system

[60] Loddo (2022).

that has multiple official languages, such as Swiss law, which is expressed in four official languages: Italian, French, German, and Romansh.

5. *Interlegal interlingual translation.* In interlegal interlingual translations, the source text and the target text are written in two different languages, and the translation concerns two different legal systems. In this type of translation, the translator must not only know both languages, but must also have adequate legal skills to detect discrepancies between the similar, but not identical, legal institutions that characterize the two different systems being examined. Comparative law studies have produced several examples of this type of translation.
6. *Supralegal interlingual translation.* Supralegal interlingual translation takes place with reference to a supralegal system and involves translating from one language to another. The Directorate General performs this type of translation for the European Commission, which has the European legal system as its reference and produces legal translations in the twenty-four languages of the EU.[61]
7. *Intralegal intersemiotic translation.* Intralegal intersemiotic translation is an intersemiotic translation in which the source document and the target document refer to the same legal system.
8. *Interlegal intersemiotic translation.* Although intralegal intersemiotic translation is the most widespread form of intersemiotic legal translation, an interlegal intersemiotic translation is not impossible.[62] This type of translation compares two different legal systems by using different semiotic systems.
9. *Supralegal intersemiotic translation* uses non-verbal signs to interpret certain aspects of the EU law. For example, the legal innovations of the EU can be represented with a cartoon or a video for the purpose of disseminating legal information, highlighting the law's impact on the lives of citizens (some direct effects) and the rationale that prompted the legislator to make that specific provision (Table 2.2).[63]

---

[61] Directorate General for Translation. In: European Commission - European Commission. https://ec.europa.eu/info/departments/translation_en. Accessed 5 October 2022. "The Directorate General for Translation of the European Commission translate laws, policy papers, reports, correspondence, etc. drafted by or sent to the Commission help the Commission communicate with the public, thereby helping citizens understand EU policies edit original documents drafted by Commission authors advise Commission departments on language and on managing multilingual websites ensure correct terminology in all official EU languages, as documented in the interinstitutional database IATE."

[62] An example of interlegal intersemiotic translation is the "Visual Guide for Syrian Refugees" created by the MADRE association and the CUNY Law School. It is a visual guide aimed at informing refugees from Syria about the importance of the registration of births and marriages, and provides information about the resources available in the destination countries; specifically, Lebanon, Turkey, and Jordan.

[63] We can find many examples of these videos in the official YouTube channels of the European institutions.

Table 2.2 Typologies of legal translations

Translation	Intralegal	Interlegal	Supralegal
INTERLINGUAL (translation proper)	INTERLINGUAL Intralegal	INTERLINGUAL Interlegal	INTERLINGUAL Supralegal
INTRALINGUAL (rewording)	INTRALINGUAL Intralegal	INTRALINGUAL Interlegal	INTRALINGUAL Supralegal
INTERSEMIOTIC	INTERSEMIOTIC Intralegal	INTERSEMIOTIC Interlegal	INTERSEMIOTIC Supralegal

2.4 Conclusion

This chapter provided an introductory overview of a theory of intersemiotic legal translation.

In particular, without claiming to be exhaustive, it considered both the debate that has developed among semioticians regarding intersemiotic translation and the peculiarities of legal translation. This specific methodological approach has led to the development of a typology of legal translation that also provides an account of three different forms of intersemiotic translation. This typology presupposes a distinction between the legal and semiotic dimensions of translation. The legal system helps to determine the understanding of the text that is translated into a particular semiotic code. However, the semiotic dimension and the legal dimension do not coincide, even though they are not entirely unrelated. A legislator can use a semiotic code to introduce a new rule into a legal system. However, the same norm could be translated using different semiotic codes; that is, it can be the object of an intersemiotic translation.

It is always necessary to bear in mind that the transposition of the original message can be partial or can exploit different semiotic codes.

As noted previously, intersemiotic legal translation encompasses a wide range of phenomena.

One possible form of classification of intersemiotic legal translations can concern the legal system to which the source and the target refer. An intersemiotic translation that refers to the same legal system is an intralegal intersemiotic translation. If the intersemiotic translation refers to different legal systems, we will have an interlegal intersemiotic translation. If the translation refers to a supranational order, we have a supranational intersemiotic translation.

References

Aguilera M (2019) Pictures, content, and normativity: the semantic of graphic rules. Phenomenology and Mind 17:136–149. https://doi.org/10.13128/pam-8032

Alcaraz Varó E, Hughes B (2002) Legal translation explained. St. Jerome Publishing, Manchester

Bajčić M (2017) New insights into the semantics of legal concepts and the legal dictionary. John Benjamins Publishing Company, Amsterdam-Philadelphia

Berger-Walliser G, Barton TD, Haapio H (2017) A collaborative and creative process: from visualization to legal design. American Business Law Journal 54:347–392. https://doi.org/10.1111/ablj.12101
Bobbio N (1993) Teoria generale del diritto. Giappichelli, Torino
Brunschwig CR (2021) Visual law and legal design: questions and tentative answers. Jusletter-IT. https://doi.org/10.38023/8b70bb88-de0c-4034-a54c-68409bb9549e
Cao D (2007) Law, language and translation. In: Translating law. Multilingual Matters, Bristol
Cao D (2013) Legal translation. In: Chapelle CA (ed) The encyclopedia of applied linguistics. Blackwell Publishing Ltd, Oxford. https://doi.org/10.1002/9781405198431.wbeal0679
Cheng L, Sin K-K, Cheng W (2014) Legal translation: a sociosemiotic approach. Semiotica 201: 17–33. https://doi.org/10.1515/sem-2014-0019
Conte AG (1976) Codici deontici. In: Intorno al 'codice'. Atti del terzo convegno della Associazione italiana di studi semiotici (AISS). Pavia, 1975. La Nuova Italia, Firenze, pp 13–25
Dudek M (2022) Redundancies of traffic signs: an exploratory study. Semiotica 247:283–317. https://doi.org/10.1515/sem-2020-0128
Dusi N (2015) Intersemiotic translation: theories, problems, analysis. Semiotica 206:181–205. https://doi.org/10.1515/sem-2015-0018
Dworkin R (1988) Law's empire. Harvard University Press, Cambridge
Eco U (2001) Experiences in translation. University of Toronto Press, Toronto
Giacomin J (2015) What is human centered design? The Design Journal 17:606–623. https://doi.org/10.2752/175630614X14056185480186
Goretti C (1930) I fondamenti del diritto. Libreria editrice lombarda, Milano
Gorlée DL (2004) On translating signs: exploring text and Semio-translation. Rodopi, Amsterdam-New York
Haapio H, Hagan M (2016) Design Patterns for Contracts. In: Networks. Proceedings of the 19th International Legal Informatics Symposium IRIS 2016. Österreichische Computer Gesellschaft OCG, Wein
Haapio H, Passera S (2021) Contracts as interfaces: exploring visual representation patterns in contract design. In: Katz DM, Dolin R, Bommarito M (eds) Legal informatics. Cambridge University Press, Cambridge, pp 213–238
Haapio H, Barton TD, Corrales Compagnucci M (2020) Legal design for the common good: proactive legal care by design. SSRN Journal. https://doi.org/10.2139/ssrn.3590040
Hagan MD (2018) A human-centered design approach to access to justice: generating new prototypes and hypotheses for intervention to make courts user-friendly. Indiana Journal of Law and Social Equality 6:199–239
Hage JC, von der Pfordten D (eds) (2009) Concepts of law. Springer, Dordrecht
Hart HLA (1961) The concept of law, third edition 2012. Oxford University Press, Oxford
Harvey M (2004) What's so special about legal translation? META 47:177–185. https://doi.org/10.7202/008007ar
Incampo A (1997) Atto e Funzione. Adriatica Editrice, Bari
Jakobson R (1959) On linguistic aspects of translation. In: Brower RA (ed) On translation. MIT Press, London, pp 232–239
Jakobson R (1971a) On linguistic aspects of translation. In: Selected writings II word and language. Mouton, The Hague-Paris, pp 260–266
Jakobson R (1971b) Linguistic types of aphasia. In: Selected writings. Mouton, The Hague-Paris, pp 307–333
Jakobson R (1971c) Aphasia as a linguistic topic. In: Selected writings. Mouton, The Hague-Paris, pp 229–238
Jia H (2017) Roman Jakobson's triadic division of translation revisited. Chinese Semiotic Studies 13:31–46. https://doi.org/10.1515/css-2017-0003
Lauzière L (1979) Un vocabulaire juridique bilingue canadien. META 24:109–114. https://doi.org/10.7202/003422ar

Lazzaro G (1997) Law and ordinary language. In: Jori M, Pintore A (eds) Law and language. The analytical school. Deborah Charles Publications, Liverpool, pp 175–209

Loddo OG (2020) The background of normative pictures. ARSP 106:563. https://doi.org/10.25162/arsp-2020-0023

Loddo OG, Addis A, Lorini G (2022) Intersemiotic translation of contracts into digital environments. Frontiers in Artificial Intelligence 5: 1–16

Lorini G (2019) Corporeal drawn norms. An investigation of graphic normativity in the material world of everyday objects. Phenomenology and Mind 17:80–90. https://doi.org/10.13128/pam-8027

Lorini G, Moroni S (2020) How to make norms with drawings: an investigation of normativity beyond the realm of words. Semiotica 2020:55–76. https://doi.org/10.1515/sem-2018-0062

Lorini G, Moroni S, Loddo OG (2021) Deontic artifacts. Investigating the normativity of objects. Philosophical Explorations 24:185–203. https://doi.org/10.1080/13869795.2021.1908584

Mac Aodha M (2014) Legal translation - an impossible task? Semiotica 201: 207–221. https://doi.org/10.1515/sem-2014-0017

Maynard P (2017) Drawn norms: the example of traffic signs. In: Lecis P, Lorini G, Busacchi V et al (eds) Truth, image, normativity. Quodlibet, Macerata, pp 327–352

Moroni S, Lorini G (2017) Graphic rules in planning: a critical exploration of normative drawings starting from zoning maps and form-based codes. Planning Theory 16:318–338. https://doi.org/10.1177/1473095216656389

Mounin G (1970) Introduction à la semiologie. Éditions de Minuit, Paris

Nord C (1997) Translating as a purposeful activity: functionalist approaches explained. St. Jerome Publishing, Manchester

Pintore A (1990) La teoria analitica dei concetti giuridici. Jovene, Napoli

Plaza J (1987) Tradução intersemiótica. Perspectiva, São Paulo

Queiroz J, Aguiar D (2015) C. S. Peirce and Intersemiotic Translation. In: Trifonas P. P. (eds) International Handbook of Semiotics. Springer, Dordrecht, pp 201–215

Ricca M (2023) Intercultural spaces of Law: translating invisibilities. Springer, Cham

Rotman E (1995) The inherent problems of legal translation. Indiana International & Comparative Law Review 6:187–196

Sacco R (1994) La traduzione giuridica. In: Scarpelli U, Di Lucia P (eds) Il linguaggio del diritto. LED, Milano

Sacco R (2000) Lingua e diritto. Ars interpretandi 5:117–134

Šarčević S (1997) New approach to legal translation. Kluwer, The Hague

Šarčević S (2000) Legal translation and translation theory: a receiver-oriented approach. In: La Traduction Juridique: Histoire, Théorie(s) et Pratique, 13. International Colloquium University of Geneva, February 17–19. ASTTI, Berne

Scarpelli U (1995) Il linguaggio giuridico: un ideale illuministico. In: Di Lucia P (ed) Nomografia. Linguaggio e redazione delle leggi. Giuffrè, Milano, pp 6–29

Scollon R, Scollon SW (2003) Discourses in place: language in the material world. Routledge, London

Studnicki F (1970) Traffic signs. Semiotica 2:151–172

Tarello G (1974) Il linguaggio precettivo. In: Diritto, enunciati, usi. Studi per una teoria del diritto. Il Mulino, Bologna, pp 134–142

Tijus C, Barcenilla J, de Lavalette BC, Meunier J-G (2007) The design, understanding and usage of pictograms. In: Written Documents in the Workplace, Brill

Torop P (2000) Intersemiosis and intersemiotic translation.European journal for semiotic studies 12:71–100

Vermeer H (1978) Ein Rahmen für eine allgemeine Translationstheorie. Lebende Sprachen 23:99–102

Vermeer H (1998) Starting to unask what translatology is about. Target 10:41–68

Wagner A (2006) The rules of the road, a universal visual semiotics. International Journal for the Semiotics of Law 19:311–324. https://doi.org/10.1007/s11196-006-9025-x

Wróblewski J (1986) Le problème de la traduction juridique. In: Rapports polonaise présentés au XIIe Congrès international de droit comparé. Ossolineum, Wroclaw-Warzawa-Krakôw-Gdansk-Lôdz

Chapter 3
Intersemiotic Legal Translation: Four Dimensions

Check for updates

3.1 Introduction

Translation consists of two fundamental elements: a source, which is the subject of the translation, and a target, which is the result. The translation process always involves the transformation of a source into a target. However, there are two types of translation, namely source-oriented and target-oriented translations.[1]

In source-oriented translations, as the name implies, the structure of the source is seen as the main element, and is used as a benchmark for measuring the quality of any translation based on it.

It is interesting that, in the general theory of translation, the attention has shifted from the source text to the target text. The target text has increasingly acquired autonomy with regard to the source text,[2] and the structure of the source text is no longer considered to be the ultimate guide. According to this view, the source text is relegated to the background in the translation process while the target text and its potential addressees are foregrounded; therefore, recent models have emphasized the target text and its communicative capacity.[3] As we have seen (see Sect. 2.2.3), the target text can even serve a different purpose from that of the source text.[4]

---

[1] Eco (2003a), p. 88.

[2] For a brief surrey of the strategies used in translation, see Sun (2012).

[3] The development of target-oriented translation has also led to the development of corpus-based translation techniques. In this case, when making translation choices, the translator refers to blocks of translated texts belonging to the linguistic and cultural context to which the target text is addressed. This makes it possible to facilitate and standardize the criteria adopted in the translation. This strategy is also adopted to facilitate automatic translations. In fact, contemporary machine translation systems are trained using large quantities of translated texts. A corpus is therefore a useful tool for both human and machine translation. For more about this subject, see Fantinuoli et al. (2015).

[4] Šarčević (1997); see also Engberg (2002), p. 382.

O. G. Loddo, *Intersemiotic Legal Translation*, Law and Visual Jurisprudence 11,
https://doi.org/10.1007/978-3-031-44184-4_3

Intersemiotic translation is generally target oriented. As a result of the different semiotic systems that are used, it is very difficult for the translator to orient the translation in such a way that ensures high semantic equivalence between the source and the target.

This chapter discusses four dimensions, four levels of analysis, of intersemiotic legal translations pertaining to the relationship between the source and the target.

The intersemiotic dimension refers to the transposition from one semiotic system (such as verbal language) to another semiotic system (such as visual or gestural language). Following a brief reflection on the concept of the semiotic system, this chapter focuses on translation as interpretation. The creative dimension is also the subject of analysis as it is an essential element of translation, as well as due to its relevance and its impact on the quality of intersemiotic and interlingual translations. Finally, attention is drawn to the role and significance of multimodality in intersemiotic translations, which entails the examination of multimodal law.

3.2 The Intersemiotic Dimension

By definition, intersemiotic translation, takes place among semiotic systems that are inherently different. As a result, the target artifact is expressed using signs that belong to a semiotic system other than that of the source artifact.

The focus on the intersemiotic dimension of intersemiotic translation is fundamental for defining the concept of intersemiotic translation by highlighting both the limitations and the possibilities related to it.

Semiotic systems are systems of signs and structural patterns for constructing and deciphering messages. Linguists have attempted to identify codes in both verbal languages and in non-linguistic semiotic systems. Models of codes were regarded as the core of the development of semiotics.[5] An essential feature that differentiates intersemiotic translations from other forms of translation is that intersemiotic translations involve at least two semiotic systems that are different from each other. To better understand the mechanisms underlying intersemiotic translation, it is important to establish when we can say that two semiotic systems are different.

Jakobson appears to have left the identification of the distinctive elements of semiotic systems to the free interpretation of the reader, and limited himself to providing only a few examples. As mentioned previously, according to Jakobson, we can speak of intersemiotic transposition (or intersemiotic translation) when in translating from prose to music, dance, cinema, or painting.[6]

---

[5] Somov (2016).

[6] It should be borne in mind that some semioticians do not accept the distinction between interlingual and intersemiotic translations because they consider natural languages to be different semiotic systems and believe that translation always implies a passage from one semiotic system to another. However, the classification that Jakobson proposed presupposes a more restrictive notion of a semiotic system.

What differentiates one semiotic system from another is the channel that is used for communication. In this sense, since both the Tajik language and the English language use the verbal channel, they both refer to the same semiotic system. The semiotician Henrik Gottlieb lent support to this theory by asserting that

> all so-called natural languages, e.g., Finnish, Xhosa and Japanese are representatives of a common system: that of vocal languages ... all vocal languages use the same oral (and often written) semiotic channel.[7]

In this sense, for example, while a translation from German to English is an interlinguistic translation, the translation from vocal language to sign language is, on the other hand, an intersemiotic translation. According to Jakobson, intersemiotic translation is based on the intersemiotic "relations" that connect the different codes. In the essay *On Linguistic Types of Aphasia*, Jakobson stated that there were "various types of intersemiotic relationships, such as the transition from gestures to words, from words to gestures, from words to images, etc."[8] These relationships correspond to human abilities, some of which fail in certain forms of aphasia. The precise mechanisms underlying the nature of these abilities are complex and not yet fully understood. For example, how it is possible to identify the elements of a semiotic code of destination that are suitable for translating a message expressed in a different semiotic code is still not clear.

The theoretical notion of untranslatability appears even more compelling when considering intersemiotic translation. One may wonder whether the difference between the semiotic system of the source text and that of the target text can represent an insurmountable obstacle for the translator.

However, this clashes with the undeniable reality that translation is not only a prevalent practice in modern societies, but is also an indispensable tool in social interactions overall, and particularly in legal contexts.

Therefore, the difficulties in conceiving theoretically of the possibility of transposing a message from one semiotic system into another is in contrast to the concrete existence of intersemiotic translation practices that are aimed at facilitating some forms of legal communication through the use of non-verbal channels.

3.3 The Interpretative Dimension

Translation is not a mechanical process but involves actively interpreting the source text and conveying it in the target semiotic system. The analysis of the interpretative dimension of intersemiotic legal translation involves a critical examination of the concept of translation as interpretation, which will be discussed in the first part of

[7] Gottlieb (2017), p. 46.

[8] Jakobson (1971a), p. 330.

this paragraph. Next, we explore how intersemiotic legal translation may connect to the theories of legal interpretation.

3.3.1 *Translation as Interpretation*

The juxtaposition between the concept of *translation* and that of *interpretation* was discussed by Peirce,[9] and was subsequently adopted by Jakobson. [10]

As mentioned previously, Jakobson used the term 'interpretation' three times to define three different types of translation.[11] These three definitions exploit the ambiguity of the term interpretation.

To fully understand Jakobson's vision, it is necessary to refer to the profound influence that Peirce's philosophy had on him. Peirce himself defined translation as interpretation in several parts of his work. In particular, Peirce reiterated that the meaning of a sign was expressed by interpreting it using another sign.

However, as Eco stated, Peirce used the term translation figuratively; like a *pars pro toto*, a translation is a synecdoche of interpretation.[12]

The meaning derives from the replacement of an expression by another with similar illative consequences. In this sense, interpretation (identifying one or more meanings) is analogous to translation, which consists of saying the same thing using different signs. This interpretative process is typical of translation from one language to another, as well as of any attempt to clarify the meaning of an expression.

Peirce used the concept of translation to clarify the notion of meaning by disconnecting it from the long-standing debate between mentalists and non-mentalists.[13]

However, it is important to point out, as Eco stated, that the translator's work must not start from a semiotic system but from the interpretation of the source, the identification of its various levels of meaning, and its purposes.[14]

---

[9] See, for example, Peirce (1931) CP 5.284. Specifically, Peirce used the term translation in reference to any attribution of meaning. According to Eco (2000, pp. 56–57) the identification of translation and interpretation proposed by Peirce should not be taken literally; it would actually be a metaphorical juxtaposition, or a strategy aimed at resolving the diatribe about "where the meaning lies", whether in the mind or in behavior, for which the meaning is given when one expression is replaced by another from which all the logical (illative) consequences that follow the first also follow.

[10] For more about the influence of Peirce's thoughts on Jakobson's development of the concept of intersemiotic translation, see Queiroz and Aguiar (2015).

[11] Jakobson (1959).

[12] Eco (2000).

[13] On the nature of meaning, see the recent book by Hanks (2015).

[14] According to Eco (2003b), p. 45, "If the translation concerned only the relationships between systems, it would be necessary to agree with those who maintain that the natural language imposes on the speaker his own immeasurable vision of the world so that the translator exposes himself inevitably to failure."

The proximity between the concepts of interpretation and translation was also highlighted by hermeneutics. The hermeneutic approach emphasizes the dialogic aspect of interpretation and translation, as both interpretation and translation consist of a balance between the context of the words and their scope of application.[15]

3.3.2 *Intersemiotic Legal Translation and the Theory of Legal Interpretation*

It is possible to find a parallelism between the translation process and the interpretation of a legal text within the same legal system within the framework of the same language.[16]

As Boehme-Neßler stated:

> In the legal interpretation of texts, just like in the iconological analysis of images, there is a common goal: uncovering the various layers of meaning and understanding the deeper meaning. Hermeneutics is based on fundamental structures and basic rules, which are independent of whether it is images or texts we are attempting to understand. [17]

This parallelism should be examined carefully to avoid blind identifications.

The interpretative process at the basis of a legal translation aims to provide another text and to produce a new set of signs with similar meanings—by contrast, a legal interpretation is usually directly (or indirectly) aimed at producing legal effects through a decision.

However, the debate about the theory of legal interpretation is intertwined with the debate about legal translation, providing new perspectives for investigation that also have relevance for our inquiry regarding intersemiotic legal translation.

For example, when examining the works of textualists[18] and contextualists,[19] important questions that arise concern the legal interpreters' power, the legitimacy of the interpretive flexibility they utilize, and the degree to which the final product of the interpretive process may deviate from the original text.

---

[15] For example, Emilio Betti discussed his general theory of translation in the book *Teoria generale dell'interpertazione*. In particular, Betti considered translation to be a reproductive interpretation (*interpretazione riproduttiva*), and clearly adopted a target-oriented approach. In this regard, his criticism of Croce is particularly interesting. Betti (1990, p. 658) disavowed the bond of loyalty, as understood by Croce. According to Croce, the translator must necessarily choose between an ugly and faithful translation, and a beautiful but unfaithful translation. According to Betti, translators must prioritize the need to integrate their work into the linguistic-cultural context of the target text.

[16] Guastini (1990), p. 18.

[17] Boehme-Neßler (2011), p. 186.

[18] Scalia et al. (2018).

[19] See, for example, Dworkin (1988).

The choices made by legal translators can certainly be conditioned by (more or less) conscious theoretical considerations that can be attributed to the two approaches.[20]

Similarly to legal interpreters, legal translators need to assess the various possible legal interpretations within the legal text in the source language. According to Engberg:

> He [the translator] must be able to assess not only one of the possible contextual meanings of a text, but the relevant legal meaning of the text, i.e. the meaning that a legal practitioner would reach when reading the text.[21]

Of note, this vision, albeit with the distinctions that characterize the respective schools of thought, is shared by philosophers of the law in the analytic tradition[22] and exponents of hermeneutics.[23]

According to this perspective, legal translation and interpretation are closely connected, to the extent that they can be considered to be parts of the same operation.[24]

Both interpretation and translation involve substituting an expression with an alternative, yet semantically related, form that conveys meaning to a distinct group of recipients beyond the original addressees.[25]

Following the principles of analytic philosophy, certain legal scholars have formulated a theory suggesting that legal translation entails the interpretation of legal statements through the application of linguistic analyses.[26] These analyses involved describing the use of legal terminology and elucidating its meaning and scope.[27] According to this view, the law would have an exclusively semantic

---

[20]The questions raised by these considerations reveal deeper ontological concerns, such as the fundamental nature of the law itself, the extent to which legal meaning can be derived solely from text, and the potential limitations of textual interpretation in the context of legal analysis

[21]Engberg (2002), p. 376.

[22]According to some legal philosophers, an interpreter's speech is comparable to a translator's product, as both interpretation and translation are nothing more than reformulations of texts; see Guastini (1990); also see Mazzarese (2008).

[23]Betti (1967).

[24]This idea was stressed by the philosopher Betti, Ibid.; cf. Frosini (1994).

[25]Betti (1967), p. 6; Betti (1990), pp. 660–694.

[26]Even though the consideration appeared in a paper that Hart later disowned (Pintore 1990), it is worth mentioning Hart's (1949) consideration regarding the inherent vagueness of legal concepts and the challenges this poses for providing precise definitions or explanations. Instead, one could provide an outline of a concept based on past cases, which is how law students often begin to learn the law. Beyond a certain point, one must refer to leading cases on the subject to avoid misleading answers. For example, as Hart (1949, p. 173) stated, the question "'What is a contract?" cannot be answered by the provision of a verbal rule for the translation of a legal expression into other terms or one specifying a set of necessary and sufficient conditions." Legal concepts often require reference to specific cases and a nuanced understanding of their application.

[27]Posner (1996), p. 9.

dimension,[28] and the work of legal interpreters would consist of clarification of the interpreted text. [29]

In some cases, intersemiotic translations correspond to the abovementioned model, which is also true in the interlinguistic translation. This occurs when translators make use of signs that, even if they are not linguistic, refer to abstract concepts (such as graphs or diagrams).

However, some forms of intersemiotic legal translations, such as comics, short movies, or cartoons, are closer to the interpretative activity of a judge than they are to interlingual legal translations. A judge's interpretation is generally fact oriented and is aimed at understanding whether a particular case can be subsumed under a general or abstract rule. Intersemiotic translators can represent a norm or a legal institute via an example of its concrete application. In this case, they would imagine an exemplary yet concrete and visually representable model subsumable under the norms that they want to translate. In other words, a typical strategy of intersemiotic translation consists of exemplifying concrete instances of the norm application that could correspond to previous legal decisions or to a decision that the translators would have taken if they were the authority entrusted with implementing the norm.

3.4 The Creative Dimension

The concept of intersemiotic translation and intersemiotic transposition[30] has received particular acclaim in the field of semiotics applied to literary and artistic disciplines.[31] A famous example of intersemiotic translation is the symphonic poem *Prélude à l'après-midi d'un faune* by Claude Debussy (an intersemiotic translation of the poem *L'après-midi d'un faune* by Stéphane Mallarmé).[32] As Jakobson stated

[28] The examination of the interconnections between law and language has considerable significance in this context. For a significant scholarly contribution to the understanding of the intricate relationship between law and language, see Bobbio (1994). Also see Di Lucia (1994), who provided an illuminating survey of the existing body of literature pertaining to the interplay between law and language, and identified three different perspectives of this issue, namely law as language versus law like language, the linguistic nature of law versus the linguistic nature of norms, and the ontology of norms versus the semiotics of norms.

[29] Frosini (1994).

[30] Jakobson used the terms intersemiotic translation and intersemiotic transposition as synonyms. When describing a form of aphasia, Jakobson (1971b), p. 235 said: "Also the capacity for intersemiotic translation, i.e., transposition from one sign system to another, is missing."

[31] According to Plaza (1981), p. 45, "It is in the nature of the art to be intersemiotic; art at its extreme, the search for its purity, finds in its core the precise relations which can be set up with other systems of signs."

[32] The perspective of the *Law and Image* movement analyzed a broad spectrum of phenomena, including both the artistic representation of law and the artistic representations within legal contexts. The *Law and Image* movement succeeded in highlighting the relevance of intersemiotic translation in law in a wider sense than the one that is the focus of this book, which specifically concerns the

explicitly, it is possible only creative intersemiotic transposition "from one system of signs into another, e.g., from verbal art into music, dance, cinema, or painting." [33]

In general, intersemiotic translation always has a creative dimension. Compared to that which takes place in the other forms of translation identified by Jakobson, the translator necessarily enjoys greater freedom. This freedom is incompatible with the idea of translation as an equivalence between linguistic expressions.

The creative and interpretative dimensions are strongly linked. Based on the purpose of the translation, the translator-interpreter chooses which aspects of the source text to highlight and which to relegate to the background.

For example, intersemiotic translators exercise discretion when they select the elements to be transposed into a semiotic code that is different from the source text. In other words, the translator identifies which level of the source text must be transposed, and then adapts it to the semiotic system adopted in the translation process and to the purpose of the translation.

As Eco pointed out, intersemiotic translation presupposes a subdivision of the source text into various levels of discourse; intersemiotic translations, such as some adaptations (see Sect. 5.2.1), "isolate one of the levels of the source text." [34] The most common example is the cinematic adaptation of a novel. The movie, which is the product of an adaptation, isolates the narrative level of the novel and the sequence of events, and can omit some stylistic aspects and introduce new ones.

In other words, interpreter-translators can choose to translate one or more levels of speech; they can partially transpose the original message without necessarily affecting the quality of the translation.

The distinction among different levels of discourse is also evident in legal language. For example, an intersemiotic legal translation can (implicitly) presuppose the distinction between *sanction-stipulating rules* and rules *prescribing a specific behavior*.[35] These rules can be interpreted as two different dimensions of the same legal norm. Therefore, an intersemiotic translator can decide to focus the translation on the obligation addressed to citizens, such as by graphically representing what

---

analysis of intersemiotic translation in legal documents and intersemiotic translation that refers to legal documents. In this broader framework, this movement has succeeded in highlighting the relevance of intersemiotic legal translation through the analysis of legal iconology by pointing out how visual and other non-verbal elements can influence legal communication and interpretation, and by exploring the different relationships among law and visual culture. In particular, Douzinas explored legal iconology by focusing on the use of images in law and on the symbolic meanings they conveyed, as well as how images, gestures, and other forms of non-linguistic communication could shape our understanding of legal concepts. In general, both Douzinas and Goodrich have contributed to a broader understanding of legal communication as a complex interplay among different modes of expression, thus illuminating the ways in which jurisprudence must take not only language but also images, symbols, and other forms of non-linguistic legal communication into account. See, for example, Douzinas (1999) and Goodrich (2009, 2013). Also see Heritier (2014).

[33] Jakobson (1959), p. 238.

[34] Eco (2001), p. 125.

[35] This distinction has been addressed in different ways by different legal theorists. See, among others, Kelsen (1979, pp. 56–57) and Alf Ross (1968, pp. 91–92).

should and should not be done. The translator can also adopt a different approach and represent the sanction as a consequence of the offense. For example, in the classic "no smoking" sign, the rule prescribing a specific behavior is represented in graphic form. At the same time, the verbal text, which generally appears under the regulatory image, often includes both the prescribed behavior and the sanctions that will be imposed in the event of deviations from that behavior. This consideration is valid both if it is believed that the "no smoking" sign is a real rule and if it is seen as the graphic representation of a pre-existing rule that is expressed linguistically.

It should be clarified that the creative dimension is not an exclusive characteristic of intersemiotic translation. Furthermore, the translator can play an interpretative-creative role in interlingual translations.[36] However, in interlingual translations, this approach tends to be constrained by the need to maintain a stronger connection to the source text, while this becomes more important in intersemiotic translations.

According to Eco,

> [i]n translation proper, there is an implicit law: The ethical obligation to respect what the author has written.[37]

The work of intersemiotic translators often consists of the creation of a new artifact, which is the product of an interpretation of the source text, conveyed via signs belonging to a semiotic code that is different from that of the source text. In this case, the translator must master both codes and be able to exploit their peculiarities creatively.

The creative dimension of intersemiotic translation is one of the most problematic aspects when considering intersemiotic legal translation. Intersemiotic legal translation not only necessarily determines a partial representation of the source text, but can also be enriched with new content (more or less consciously) by the translator. For example, let us consider an animation that illustrates a new legal provision. Similarly to literary adaptations, the translator must select the level of the normative text in intersemiotic legal translations. For example, in the case of a video for the purpose of disseminating information, it could highlight the law's impact on the lives of citizens (some direct effects) and the rationale that prompted the legislator to make that specific provision. Identifying a single ratio in a legislative text, approved by hundreds of parliamentarians for the most diverse reasons, is a stretch. An official justification for encouraging the application of the rule appears to be much more likely to be highlighted, but it may have ideological connotations.

Some parts of the legislation could be clarified through examples of the application thereof. This does not prevent other parts, which are difficult to represent because they are technically more complex, from being neglected by the translator and then re-emerging at the time of the actual application of the rule or in the context of a dispute. However, in some cases, an intersemiotic translation could facilitate citizens' knowledge about and understanding of the norms.

---

[36] Eco (2001), p. 126.

[37] Eco (2003a), p. 3.

3.5 The Multimodal Dimension

In the book *Tradução intersemiótica,* the Brazilian semiotician Plaza emphasized the role of multimodality in intersemiotic translations. The theory of intersemiotic translation proposed by Plaza focused particularly on art studies, and was thus more concerned with intergenic transmutations (such as pictorial, photographic, cinematographic, graphic, and musical transmutations) than exclusively with the passage from linguistic to non-linguistic signs systems. Although Plaza's research focused on art studies, which are outside of the scope of this book, it is nonetheless intriguing to find constant references to multimodal artifacts in his book. Some legal design scholars have seriously considered the application of multimodal communication to the legal sphere; [38] among the phenomena they describe are some examples of intersemiotic translation. Others seem to consider an overlap between intersemiotic translation and multimodality. [39] Therefore, it is important to clarify the relevance of multimodality in intersemiotic translation, what binds the two phenomena together, and what differentiates them.[40]

3.5.1 Intersemiotic Translation Versus Multimodality: A Conceptual Clarification

The term multimodality refers to the coordination of multiple different systems of signs to communicate a single, or at least unified, message or meaning.

According to the linguist and semiotician Gunther Kress, "multimodality is the normal state of communication." [41]

In fact, we often encounter examples of multimodal communication in our daily lives, some of which are forms of intersemiotic legal translation. For example, if we are not disciplined drivers, we can encounter a traffic policeman who, being endowed with legally recognized authority, orders us to stop via an acoustic signal (a whistle) accompanied by a visual signal (a gesture).

Not all multimodal messages are intersemiotic translations. The two phenomena must not be confused. 'I ♥ Cagliari' embroidered on a scarf worn by a supporter of a certain football team is, of course, multimodal, but it is not an intersemiotic translation *per se*. In fact, in this example, there is not necessarily a relationship with a source text.

[38] Brunschwig (2019).

[39] Pitkäsalo et al. (2022).

[40] Plaza (1987), pp. 66–67.

[41] Kress (2010a), p. 2.

As mentioned previously, an intersemiotic legal translation does not necessarily require a complete transposition of the source text into the target text. Furthermore, the two texts need not be completely independent of each other.

Even if the multimodal text is not necessarily an intersemiotic translation, the target text of an intersemiotic translation can be a multimodal text. In other words, some verbal legal texts can be translated into multimodal target texts. For example, a traditional verbal contract can be translated intersemiotically into a comic contract. A comic contract is undoubtedly multimodal (it combines images and writing), and is simultaneously the intersemiotic legal translation of a traditional contract expressed exclusively in verbal form. [42]

Multimodality is an extremely important tool for making some forms of intersemiotic translation possible. We have seen that some non-linguistic semiotic systems have clear limitations in terms of accounting for legal or normative meanings, which can only be conveyed through words.

Moreover, a multimodal target text of an intersemiotic translation is often characterized by *intersemiotic redundancies*; that is, redundancies expressing the same meaning of a part of the source text within the same document using different semiotic tools. These forms of redundancies may occur in legal texts. For example, European lawmakers (in the General Data Protection Regulation) approve of the use of icons in privacy policies. These icons are used to highlight content that has already been expressed in the verbal part of the policy. Instead of adding a new meaning to the privacy policy, they reinterpreted it using graphic codes. Finally, an intersemiotic translation may be displayed in a document that is not multimodal. It is a somewhat difficult phenomenon to exemplify in the legal field, but it is the most elementary form of intersemiotic translation. This occurs when both the target text and the source text are monomodal; for example, a verbal text that is translated into drawings (Figs. 3.1 and 3.2). As Jakobson stated,

> [t]he study of communication must distinguish between homogeneous messages which use a single semiotic system and syncretic messages based on a combination or merger of different sign patterns. [43]

3.5.2 *Multiple Semiotic Resources*

Intersemiotic translations make a message available by exploiting different semiotic resources, such as signals, indicators, expressions, gestures, or other types of signs, symbols, and their interconnections. [44]

Although the concept of intersemiotic translation does not coincide with that of multimodality, the two strategies for creating meaning share a pragmatic

[42] Pitkäsalo et al. (2022).

[43] Jakobson (1971c), p. 705.

[44] Pârlog (2019), p. 21.

INFORMATIVA RELATIVA AL TRATTAMENTO DEI DATI PERSONALI AI SENSI DEL REGOLAMENTO EUROPEO 2016/679

CATEGORIA DI INTERESSATI: STUDENTI

Questa informativa viene fornita ai sensi dell'art. 13 del Regolamento EU 2016/679 (di seguito anche Regolamento); il trattamento sarà improntato ai principi di correttezza, liceità e trasparenza e di tutela della Sua riservatezza e dei Suoi diritti.

Titolare del trattamento	**Denominazione Sociale:**	Università degli Studi di Cagliari
	Indirizzo:	Via Università, 40 - 09124 Cagliari
	Indirizzo e-mail:	privacy@unica.it
	PEC:	protocollo@pec.unica.it
Responsabile della protezione dei dati (RPD)	**Indirizzo e-mail:**	dpo@unica.it
	PEC:	protocollo@pec.unica.it

Soggetti autorizzati al trattamento

I Dati potranno essere trattati dal personale delle strutture di Ateneo deputate al perseguimento delle finalità sotto indicate, che sono stati espressamente autorizzati al trattamento e che hanno ricevuto adeguate istruzioni operative.

Misure di sicurezza

Il titolare del trattamento la informa che il trattamento dei suoi dati è effettuato con strumenti prevalentemente automatizzati adottando misure di sicurezza tali da garantire la tutela e la massima riservatezza dei dati trattati. In occasione del Trattamento dei Suoi dati, il Titolare potrebbe venire a conoscenza anche di dati che il Codice definisce particolari, quali, a titolo esemplificativo, quelli idonei a rivelare lo stato di salute, l'appartenenza ad organizzazioni religiose, politiche o sindacali, giudiziari. Anche a tale riguardo Le confermiamo che tali dati verranno trattati con la massima riservatezza e nel pieno rispetto delle disposizioni di legge.

Finalità del trattamento	**Base giuridica del trattamento**
Finalità	**Base Giuridica del Trattamento**
ACCESSO AI CORSI DI STUDIO	Compito di interesse pubblico o connesso all'esercizio di pubblici poteri
ACCOGLIENZA	Compito di interesse pubblico o connesso all'esercizio di pubblici poteri
ACCORDI/CONVENZIONI	Compito di interesse pubblico o connesso all'esercizio di pubblici poteri
ACCORDI/CONVENZIONI CON ALTRI ATENEI O ENTRI PUBBLICI E PRIVATI - MASTER	Compito di interesse pubblico o connesso all'esercizio di pubblici poteri
ACCREDITAMENTO INIZIALE E ATTIVAZIONE CORSI DI STUDIO	Compito di interesse pubblico o connesso all'esercizio di pubblici poteri , Consenso dell'interessato

Fig. 3.1 A privacy policy of the University of Cagliari illustrated using icons. Student's Privacy Policy University of Cagliari https://web.unica.it/unica/protected/423459/0/def/ref/GNC139335/. Accessed 02 October 2023. Used with permission. Courtesy of the University of Cagliari

assumption; that is, both a creator of multimodal texts and an intersemiotic translator intend to exploit the semiotic resources available in order to facilitate the communication process. According to van Leeuwen:

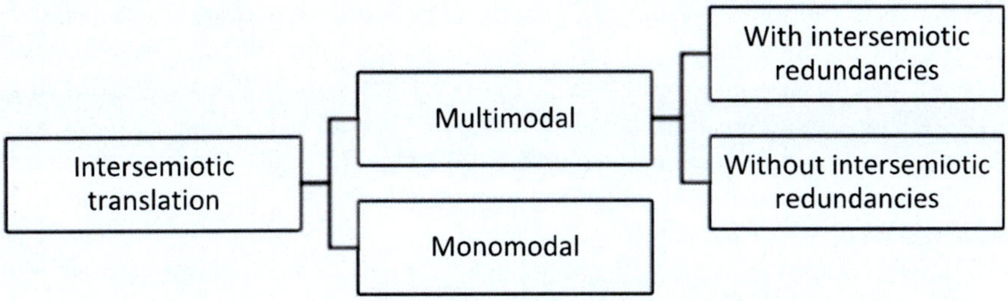

Fig. 3.2 An outline of the possible relationships among multimodality and intersemiotic translations

> Semiotic resources are the actions, materials, and artifacts we use for communicative purposes, whether produced physiologically–for example, with our vocal apparatus, the muscles we use to make facial expressions and gestures–or technologically–for example, with pen and ink, or computer hardware and software–together with the ways in which these resources can be organized. Semiotic resources have a meaning potential, based on their past uses, and a set of affordances based on their possible uses, and these will be actualized in concrete social contexts where their use is subject to some form of semiotic regime. [45]

Kress emphasized that these resources mutated constantly. People, as sign-makers, shape and combine semiotic resources according to their interests. This concept is a shift away from conventional notions of grammar that consider communication as reproducing existing signs within a relatively stable and fixed system of choices.[46]

As Kress stated,

> [m]ultimodality includes questions around the potentials–the affordances–of the resources that are available in any one society for the making of meaning; and how, therefore, 'knowledge' appears differently in different modes.[47]

Images and gestures have been part of human culture for much longer than has writing. New forms of communication have developed due to an interconnected web of social, economic, cultural, and technological changes. Semiotic effects are evident in various domains, including the legal one. At the level of semiotic production, there has been a marked shift from paper documents to the screen. Furthermore, the move from paper to screen has also encouraged the transition from a single mode of communication to multimodal communication in the legal field.

The development and exploitation of various semiotic resources can be promoted or hindered by social factors.

In other words, technological development and its impact on daily communication have encouraged the exploitation of images, as well as other semiotic resources that are combined with the needs of digital communication. However, precisely because the use of certain communication tools has a social dimension, their

[45] Van Leeuwen (2005), p. 285.

[46] Kress (2010a).

[47] Kress (2010b), p. 38.

adoption is conditioned by the rules and traditions of the various socio-cultural spheres and by the traditions of certain social groups. This applies particularly to the legal sphere. As mentioned by the legal sociologist Volker Boehme-Neßler, the legal field appears to be affected by a logocentric prejudice.[48]

To use multimedia technologies effectively, writers need to employ practices that are not only verbal, but which are also visual, spatial, aural, and gestural to make meaning.

In fact, forms of multimodal legal communications are beginning to spread and deserve to be explored. In order to do so, jurisprudence and legal practice would need to draw on various legal and non-legal disciplines. [49]

3.6 Conclusion

The analysis of the four dimensions outlined above revealed that some conceptual tools developed in the fields of philosophy of language and philosophy of law could be applied to intersemiotic translations in the legal field. Therefore, there are conditions of translatability that, if satisfied, allow for the transposition of a source legal text using a different semiotic system.

Pansemiotic features are common to all semiotic systems. As Jakobson stated,

> [l]anguage shares many properties with some systems of signs, other properties are instead present in all systems of signs.[50]

In order for an intersemiotic translation to be possible, it must be possible for there to be a relationship between the source text and the target text on at least one level. This relationship can concern the semantic level, the pragmatic level, and the syntactic level.

The identification of similar characteristics in different semiotic systems has already been widely investigated. With regard to the legal field, in the essay *Traffic Signs*, [51] the Polish jurist Franciszek Studnicki stated that the iconic system of road signs and verbal language, despite being different semiotic systems, both possessed syntax, semantics, and vocabulary. The traffic sign system was created to communicate relevant normative information about a road's conditions to foreigners. In this regard, as the semiotician Krampen stated,

> [p]ictures or 'icons' are used in [...] a sign system precisely because the international necessity for such a system makes supra-linguistic means essential.[52]

---

[48] Boehme-Neßler (2011).

[49] Svantesson and Brunschwig (2013), p. 272.

[50] Jakobson (1960), p. 351.

[51] Studnicki (1970).

[52] Krampen (1983).

In fact, even though both conventional signs and iconic signs need to be learned, the rules expressed in pictograms can be easier to understand than their linguistic formulations.

This is well known by semioticians who have analyzed the structure (syntax), meaning (semantics), and usage (pragmatics) of this system of signs. [53]

The semantic level concerns a correspondence between the source and the target in relation to the meaning; the pragmatic level concerns an association between the function of the source text and that of the target text which, as we have seen, does not necessarily exist, while the syntactic aspect pertains to the relationships among signs and the possibility of combining them to create an argument.

If we consider the intersemiotic translation from verbal to visual language, we can see that both verbal language and visual systems can combine (more or less) articulated signs and can transmit information. Such combinations of signs may have propositional content.[54]

A translation should be able to transpose the logical relationships that are present in the source text, at least in part.

Therefore, the problem that arises is identifying a correspondence between the logical relations that can be represented using the original semiotic system and those that can be represented via the system that is used in the translation. The idea that non-linguistic semiotic systems cannot reproduce the logical relations that are present in language may lead us to think that intersemiotic translation is, in fact, impossible.[55]

Some scholars have argued that paintings, drawings, and images do not have fixed syntactic structures; that is, they are not composed of a fixed set of primitive symbols or a set of formation rules.

However, there are several widespread visual communication strategies that have been adopted systematically. These strategies are characterized by precise and defined grammars. For example, in his book *Envisioning Information,* Tufte[56] refers to the rules presented in Eduard Imhof's book, *Cartographic Relief Presentation*.[57] These rules were not only aimed at facilitating the understanding of the message by the recipient, but also aimed to propose techniques to reproduce logical relationships in graphic form.

From a logical point of view, the difference between two semiotic systems, and particularly between the visual semiotic system and the linguistic one, is the basis of the debate concerning the possibility of presenting an argument through images. For a long time, it was believed that logical relationships referred exclusively to relationships between sentences. However, if we consider logic as a general theory of the fundamental relationships among our representations of the world, we can admit the

[53] See Ibid., p. 168; Tijus et al. (2007), p. 25.

[54] Tijus et al. (2007).

[55] See Aguilera (2019); Camp (2007).

[56] Tufte (1990), p. 82.

[57] Imhof (2007)

possibility that these relationships can be reproduced in non-linguistic semiotic systems; for example, those composed of images.[58]

Intersemiotic translation presupposes the possibility of reproducing the logical relationships that are outlined in the source text, at least in part.

References

Aguilera M (2019) Pictures, content, and normativity: the semantic of graphic rules. Phenomenology and Mind 17:136–149. https://doi.org/10.13128/pam-8032

Betti E (1967) Traduzione e interpretazione. Responsabilità del sapere 81:1–36

Betti E (1990) Teoria generale della interpretazione. Giuffrè, Milano

Bobbio N (1994) Scienza del diritto e analisi del linguaggio [1950]. In: Scarpelli U, Di Lucia P (eds) Il linguaggio del diritto. LED, Milano

Boehme-Neßler V (2011) Pictorial Law. Modern law and the power of pictures. Springer, Berlin

Brunschwig CR (2019) Perspectives of digital law: visualization, audiovisualization, and multisensorization. SSRN Journal. https://doi.org/10.2139/ssrn.3795146

Camp E (2007) Thinking with maps. Philos Perspect 21:145–182

Di Lucia P (1994) Introduction. In: Scarpelli U, Di Lucia P (eds) Il linguaggio del diritto. LED, Milano

Douzinas C (1999) Law and the image. Gramma: J Theory Criticism 7:15–39. https://doi.org/10.26262/GRAMMA.V7I0.7309

Dworkin R (1988) Law's empire. Belknap Press, Cambridge

Eco U (2000) Traduzione e interpretazione. Quaderni di studi semiotici 85/86/87:55–100

Eco U (2001) Experiences in translation. University of Toronto Press, Toronto

Eco U (2003a) Mouse or Rat? Translation as negotiation. Phoenix, London

Eco U (2003b) Dire quasi la stessa cosa: Esperienze di traduzione. Bompiani, Milano

Engberg J (2002) Legal meaning assumptions - what are the consequences for legal interpretation and legal translation? International Journal for the Semiotics of Law 15:375–388

Fantinuoli C, Zanettin F, Doms S et al (2015) New directions in corpus-based translation studies. Language Science Press

Frosini V (1994) Traduzione e interpretazione dei testi giuridici nel pensiero di Emilio Betti. In: Frosini V, Ricobono F (eds) L'ermeneutica giuridica di Emilio Betti. Giuffrè, Milano

Goodrich P (2009) Screening law. Law Liter 21:1–23. https://doi.org/10.1525/lal.2009.21.1.1

Goodrich P (2013) Visiocracy: on the futures of the fingerpost. Critical Inquiry 39:498–530

Gottlieb H (2017) Semiotics and translation. In: Malmkjær K (ed) The Routledge handbook of translation studies and linguistics, 1st edn. Routledge

Guastini R (1990) Dalle fonti alle norme. Giappichelli, Torino

Hanks P (2015) Propositional content. Oxford University Press, Oxford

Hart HLA (1949) The Ascription of Responsibility and Rights. Proceedings of the Aristotelian Society, New Series 4:171–194

Heritier P (2014) Estetica giuridica inclusiva vs. positivismo esclusivo. L'immagine nel sistema delle fonti e i nomogrammi. In: Faralli C, Heritier P, Faralli C et al (eds) Il diritto tra testo e immagine. Rappresentazione delle fonti. Mimesis, Milano-Udine, pp 55–70

Imhof E (2007) Cartographic relief presentation. ESRI

Jakobson R (1959) On linguistic aspects of translation. In: Brower RA (ed) On translation. MIT Press, London, pp 232–239

[58] Westerhoff (2005).

Jakobson R (1960) Closing statement: linguistics and poetics. In: Sebeok T (ed) Style in language. MIT Press, New York-London, p 15
Jakobson R (1971a) Linguistic types of aphasia. In: Selected writings. Mouton, The Hague-Paris, pp 307–333
Jakobson R (1971b) Aphasia as a linguistic topic. In: Selected writings. Mouton, The Hague-Paris, pp 229–238
Jakobson R (1971c) Language in relation to other communication systems. In: Selected writings. Mouton, The Hague-Paris, pp 697–708
Kelsen H (1979) General Theory of Norms. Clarendon, Oxford, 1991
Krampen M (1983) Icons of the road. Semiotica 43:1–204
Kress G (2010a) Multimodality. A social semiotic approach to contemporary communication. Routledge, London
Kress G (2010b) Multimodal discourse analysis. In: The Routledge handbook of discourse analysis. Routledge, London, New York
Mazzarese T (2008) Interpretazione e traduzione del diritto nello spazio giuridico globale. Diritto e questioni pubbliche 88:88–102
Pârlog A-C (2019) Intersemiotic translation: literary and linguistic multimodality. Palgrave Macmillan, Cham
Peirce CS (1931) The collected papers of Charles Sanders Peirce. Harvard University Press, Cambridge
Pintore A (1990) La teoria analitica dei concetti giuridici. Jovene, Napoli
Pitkäsalo E, Ketola A, Haavisto V, Kalliomaa-Puha L (2022) Image analysis as a visualization tool - translating contracts into comics. In: Corrales Compagnucci M, Haapio H, Fenwick M (eds) Research handbook on contract design. Edward Elgar Publishing, Northampton, pp 347–364
Plaza J (1981) Reflection of and on theories of translation. Dispostio 6:55–91
Plaza J (1987) Tradução intersemiótica. Perspectiva, São Paulo
Posner RA (1996) Pragmatic adjudication. Cardozo Law Review 18:1–20
Queiroz J, Aguiar D (2015) C. S. Peirce and Intersemiotic Translation. In: Trifonas P (ed) International Handbook of Semiotics. Springer, Dordrecht, pp 201–215
Ross A (1968) Directives and Norms. Routledge & K. Paul, London
Šarčević S (1997) New approach to legal translation. Kluwer, The Hague
Scalia A, Amar AR, Calabresi SG (2018) A matter of interpretation: Federal Courts and the law, New edn. Princeton University Press, Princeton
Somov GY (2016) Interrelations of codes in human semiotic systems. Semiotica 213:557–599. https://doi.org/10.1515/sem-2015-0138
Studnicki F (1970) Traffic signs. Semiotica 2:151–172
Sun S (2013) Strategies of translation. In: Chapelle CA (ed) The encyclopedia of applied linguistics. Blackwell Publishing Ltd, Oxford, pp. 5408-5412 https://doi.org/10.1002/9781405198431.wbeal1117
Brunschwig CR (2013) Law Is Not or Must Not Be Just Verbal and Visual in the 21st Century: Toward Multisensory Law. In: Svantesson DJB, Greenstein S (eds) Internationalisation of law in the digital information society, 1. ed. Ex Tuto Publ, København
Tijus C, Barcenilla J, Lavalette Cambon de B, Meunier J-G (2007) The design, understanding and usage of pictograms. In: Alamargot DJ, Terrier P, Cellier J-M (eds) Written Documents in the Workplace. Brill, pp 17–31
Tufte ER (1990) Envisioning information. Graphics Press, Cheshire
Van Leeuwen T (2005) Introducing social semiotics. Routledge, London
Westerhoff J (2005) Logical relations between pictures. The Journal of Philosophy 102:603–623

Chapter 4
Intersemiotic Legal Translation as Target *Representamen*: Three Types of Intersemiotic Translation in the Legal Field

4.1 Introduction

The term 'translation' can refer to the product of the semiotic act of translating. Following the lexicon of translation theory, we can call that product 'target text.' More precisely, since we are discussing "intersemiotic translation," a concept that was developed by Jakobson, who was strongly influenced by Peirce's philosophy, we could reframe Peirce's lexicon and call the product of the semiotic act of translating the 'target representamen.'

It is useful to remember that, according to Peirce, there are at least three elements that contribute to creating meaning (Fig. 4.1). These are

(i) representamen,
(ii) object, and
(iii) interpretant.

According to Peirce,

> [a] sign, or representamen, is something that stands to somebody for something in some respect or capacity. It addresses somebody, that is, creates in the mind of that person an equivalent sign or perhaps a more developed sign. That sign which it creates I call the interpretant of the first sign. The sign stands for something, its object. [1]

It is important to point out that both the representamen and the interpretant are signs; moreover, although both stand for an object, they could stand for the same object in different ways. In Peirce's words, the "sign stands for that object, not in all respects, but in reference to some kind of idea. The interpretant derives from the relationship between representamen and object."[2]

[1] Peirce (1931) CP 2.274.

[2] Peirce (1931) CP 2.228.

O. G. Loddo, *Intersemiotic Legal Translation*, Law and Visual Jurisprudence 11,
https://doi.org/10.1007/978-3-031-44184-4_4

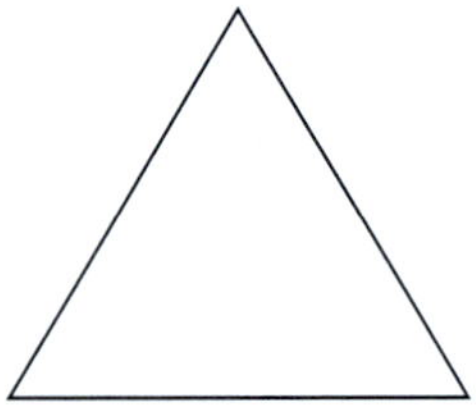

Fig. 4.1 A graphic representation of Peirce's theory of sign

Peirce intended to participate in the debate concerning the nature of "meaning." This debate will not be analyzed in this book.

What is interesting for our research purposes, which Jakobson understood perfectly, is that Peirce's concept of the sign sheds light on general translation theory.

Jakobson applied Peirce's concept of the sign (and of the meaning) to the phenomenon of translation. Signs frame both the source text and the target text and, according to Jakobson,[3] translation is an interpretation of a sign by means of other signs (see Sect. 3.3.1).

According to Peirce, we can categorize signs according to the relation of the sign to its object. We will have icons, symbols, or indices depending on whether the relation between the sign and its object consists of similarity (icon), convention (symbol), or physical contiguity (index).

The target representamen is related to the source representamen. In this sense, we could understand a translation as creating a relationship between two representamens, thus highlighting one of the essential characteristics of the translation. Both the source representamen and the target representamen relate to an object (Fig. 4.2). The idea that a sign refers to an object could be criticized based on metaphysical naivety.[4] However, it is quite difficult to formulate a theory of intersemiotic translation that consists solely of relationships between signs without considering any interaction with an object.[5]

---

[3] Jakobson (1959).

[4] The idea of applying Peirce's concept of the sign to intersemiotic translation originated in Queiroz and Aguiar's (2015) work; however, their work appeared to identify translation with a single semiotic process in which the source is the interpretant and the target is the interpretamen. In fact, since there are at least two signs (source and target) in a translation, my reconstruction takes two different processes of creation of meaning and their interaction into account.

[5] Peirce (1931) CP4.536 differentiated between immediate objects (iO) and dynamic objects ($_{d}O$), and stated: "We have to distinguish the Immediate Object, which is the Object as the Sign itself represents it, and whose being is thus dependent upon the Representation of it in the Sign, from the Dynamical Object, which is the Reality which by some means contrives to determine the Sign to its Representation." The subsistence of a dynamic object is a necessary condition for the execution of a semiotic act.

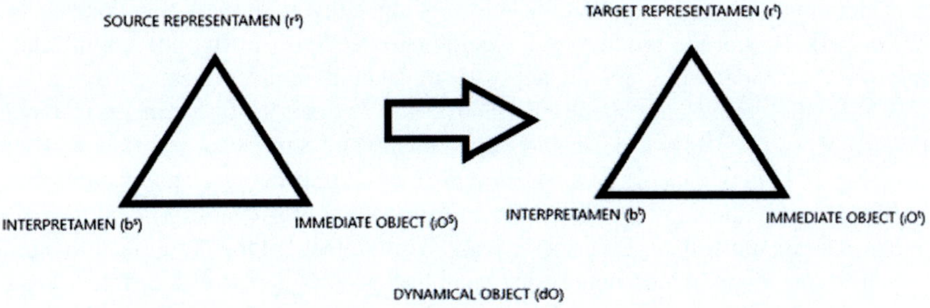

Fig. 4.2 A graphic illustration of the relationship between the source representamen and the target representamen

We can discuss not only the ontology of that object, its real or fictitious nature, but also the semiotic act; regardless of whether it is a communication or a translation, it must always have an object and must always refer to something. In the lexicon of the philosophy of mind, both an act of communication and an act of translation are intentional acts. In this sense, according to Eco,

> [w]e produce signs because there is something that demands to be said. To use an expression that is efficacious albeit not very philosophical, the Dynamical Object is Something-that-sets-to-kicking us and says "Talk!" to us—or "Talk about me!" or again, "Take me into consideration!"[6]

In fact, the term object could obscure a complex set of entities that affect sign production and cognitive processes differently. The nature of these entities can also vary: they can be material, psychological, ideal, cultural, institutional, juridical, or normative entities.[7] In general, both the source representamen and the target representamen refer to the same object in a translation; nonetheless, a different interpretant is possible, and different representamens are necessary. In this sense, in a translation:

$$^{d}O = {}^{d}O$$

$$r^{s} \neq r^{t}$$

$$i^{s} = i^{t} \vee i^{s} \neq i^{t}$$

where ^{d}O is the dynamic object, r^{s} and r^{t} are the source and the target representamen, and i^{s} and i^{t} are the source and the target interpretamen. One might think that these

[6] Eco (1999), p. 14.

[7] For a reflection on the relationship between semiotics and the ontology of the norm, see Di Lucia and Passerini Glazel (2022).

considerations only apply to the translations of signs that refer to physical objects or objects that are not the product of a specific culture. Specifically, one might think that these considerations do not apply to translations concerning legal objects.[8] However, the equivalence mentioned above also appears to occur in legal translations. More precisely, it occurs in intra-, inter-, and supralegal translations (see Sect. 2.2.2). In fact, it would be misleading to think of translating a legal institute or a legal fact;[9] only the signs that stand for an institute are translatable.

An interlegal translator describes a legal institute that belongs to a specific legal system to recipients whose conceptual legal background is part of a different legal system. In this case, a translation that is understandable to the intended addressee (s) must not take the assumptions derived from the source legal culture for granted, and must highlight the differences from that same institution in the target legal culture.

For example, let us imagine an essay that describes a decision of the French *Cour de cassation* concerning a specific institution. The essay is addressed to an audience of Italian jurists, and has been translated into Italian. In the abovementioned typology (Sect. 2.3.3), this would be an example of an interlegal-interlinguistic translation. In this case, the legal institute that is the object of the essay will certainly be the same in both in the source text and in the target text, but the translator, in order to make the French institution understandable to Italian jurists, may take both the background of the Italian jurists and the background of the French jurists into account. The translator must mediate between the two legal cultures using specific measures, such as explanatory notes aimed at clarifying the assumptions that a French jurist could take for granted, and point out the differences between the French institution and the Italian one. However, the source text and the target text have the same object.

One possible way of classifying intersemiotic translation, which focuses on the target representamen, has been delineated by the semiotician Plaza.[10] Plaza, who adopted the classification of signs introduced by Peirce, created a typology of intersemiotic translation based on the relationship between the target representamen and its object. In this regard, Plaza identified three types of intersemiotic translation:

- *Iconic* intersemiotic translation,
- *indical* intersemiotic translation, and
- *symbolic* intersemiotic translation.

In an *iconic intersemiotic translation*, the target representamen produces meaning that is derived from its similarities to the object.

[8] Lorini and Loddo (2022).

[9] In fact, legal translation must not be confused with legal transplants; for example, according to Watson (1993), p. 21, "the moving of a rule or a system of law from one country to another, or from one people to another."

[10] Plaza (1987).

In an *indical intersemiotic translation*, the meaning of the target representamen is determined by the contiguity between the object and the medium that hosts the sign.

In a *symbolic intersemiotic translation*, the target representamen relates to its object 'according to certain conventions.

Plaza's decision to use Peirce's categories as a key to reading Jakobson's semiotic translation theory was not arbitrary, as Pierce's theory of signs strongly permeated Jakobson's theory of translation.[11] As Plaza mainly applied his classification to the field of art studies, a more in-depth analysis of his work could lead us away from the actual theoretical objective of this book, namely the creation of conceptual tools that are suitable for the analysis and production of intersemiotic translations of legal documents. However, as will be shown, Plaza's proposal is also theoretically appealing due to its applicability to legal language. [12]

Another interesting application of Peirce's grammar was presented by Nicole Amare and Alan Manning in their book *A unified theory of information design.* [13] The authors created a general theory of visual information design based on Peirce's typology. Their work has elements of interest because it can provide intersemiotic translators with guidelines to facilitate the creation of effective translations from a communicative point of view. Similarly to Plaza, Amare and Manning did not focus on forms of intersemiotic translation of texts with legal content. However, some of the guidelines they provided regarding the use of different types of signs (indexes, icons, or symbols) in the context of information design can also be extremely useful for intersemiotic legal translators. Their observations could assist in establishing the conditions under which it is better to use an iconic, a symbolic, or an indexical intersemiotic translation. Starting from these premises, the distinction among iconic, symbolic, and indexical translation should become clearer. According to Plaza,

> [f]rom a semiotic point of view [. . .] languages operate and function at three levels of complexity in the process of semiosis and compliance with the characteristics of iconicity, indexicality, and symbolicity.[14]

The following paragraphs consider each of these forms of intersemiotic translations, and attempt to identify some specific examples in the legal field. In view of this typology, the chapter illustrated different strategies for intersemiotic translations concerning different target representamens such as drawings, material artifacts, and digital artifacts. Finally, the chapter investigated the complex connections between the typology of norms and the diverse target representamens in intersemiotic translations.

---

[11] Eco (2000), Eco (2001), Queiroz and Aguiar (2015), and Eco (2003b). See Sect. 2.3.

[12] As Bobbio (1993), p. 53 emphasized, language can have a *prescriptive function*, and can be a tool for influencing people's behavior; for example, through commands, advice, recommendations, and warnings. In legal translations, the target text can maintain a prescriptive function, or can have a descriptive function, and can describe norms.

[13] Amare and Manning (2013).

[14] Plaza (1987), p. 67 (my translation).

4.2 Iconic Intersemiotic Legal Translation

In an *iconic intersemiotic translation*, the target representamen is an icon; that is, it produces meaning derived from the similarities to its object.

Both the source and the target representamens may be icons. However, in the case of intersemiotic translations, it is more common for the target and source representamens to have different relationships with the object. For example, in the intersemiotic translation between the word dog and an image of a dog, the source representamen has a symbolic relationship with the object. By contrast, the target representamen has a relationship of iconicity with the object.

In Peirce's lexicon, an icon is a sign that determines the interpretant by creating a relationship of similarity with the object.

According to Peirce,

> [a] sign may be iconic; that is, it may represent its object mainly by similarity, no matter what its mode of being. This "similarity" can consist in partaking of simple qualities of the object (as in the case of images).[15]

The similarity is based on a rule of comparison that tells us how to individuate the relationship between a sign and its object. [16] This rule can be understood spontaneously by the recipient of the communication, or could be the product of conventions that highlight the aspects of the object to which one should pay attention in order to identify an iconic relationship between the object and the sign. [17]

In fact, a sign is also iconic if its likeness to the object is derived from conventional rules. In this regard, an algebraic formula is iconic because rules of change and association stipulate the distribution of the symbols surrounding the identity sign. [18]

An icon potentially refers to an indefinite class of objects, namely all those objects that have a relationship of similarity to it in some way. Some semioticians have remarked that any phenomenon can be said to be similar to any other phenomenon in some respects if the chosen criterion of similarity is sufficiently general, just as the establishment of any convention immediately implies a similarity relationship.

However, the similarity criterion can be the subject of an axiological-formal evaluation if it is sufficient for the communicative needs that the icon aims to satisfy. These criteria are generally identified via the theory of information design on which legal design draws (or should draw). [19]

In general, icons are not necessarily images. In fact, acoustic icons are possible. As Eco stated:

---

[15] Peirce (1931) CP.2.92.

[16] See Polidoro (2015), p. 155.

[17] In general, according to Peirce, icons could be images, diagrams, or metaphors.

[18] Krampen (1983), p. 6.

[19] In this sense, "[a]nything whatever, be it quality, existent individual, or law, is an Icon of anything in so far as it is like that thing and used as a sign of it." Peirce (1931) CP 2.247.

> [a]n icon is not necessarily an image in the visual sense of the term, because also the melody we whistle, perhaps tunelessly, may be an icon of Beethoven's Fifth. [20]

However, since the visual (graphics and pictograms) and verbal dimensions prevail in the legal field, we will focus our attention on them.

Diagrams are an example of visual icons; according to Peirce, they are special sorts of icons that represent the objects in terms of interrelated parts and which facilitate reasoning. According to this definition, maps, algebraic formulas, and bars or line graphs are examples of diagrams. [21]

As Peirce stated,

> [d]iagrams [. . .] are intended to be applied to the better understanding of states of things, whether experienced, or read of, or imagined. [22]

More precisely, diagrams "represent the relation [. . .] of the part of one thing by analogous relations in their [the diagrams'] own parts". [23] A diagram displays the interrelation between the parts of the object it depicts, and facilitates reasoning and thought processes. This distances the concept of interpreting signs from the idea of simple coding and decoding, and raises epistemological issues related to acquiring knowledge via signs. [24]

Studying the characteristics of iconic signs in semiotics is useful for lawyers because not only words but also pictograms and other types of iconic signs can communicate and clarify legal contents. In this regard, juxtaposing an iconic sign with a verbal legal text is a legal drafting practice that can take different forms and, consequently, can have different functions.

By 'icon,' legal designers usually mean an image that highlights and illustrates specific content related to the translated text.[25] This image is usually a pictogram characterized by a resemblance to a physical object. The legislator referred to this

---

[20] Eco (1999), p. 65. It should be emphasized that, as Eco also clarified, similarity must not be confused with resemblance. One phenomenon resembles another because it causes the same reaction in the subject.

[21] Stjernfelt (2007), p. ix.

[22] Peirce (1931) CP 3.419.

[23] Amare and Manning (2013), p. 94.

[24] Stjernfelt, starting from Peirce's semiotics, investigated the role of diagrams for thought and knowledge. Based on the general doctrine of diagrams in Peirce's mature work, diagrammatology claims that diagrams constitute a centerpiece of epistemology. Stjernfelt, following Peirce, differentiated among (i) signs referring to qualities and verbs, (ii) signs referring to subjects related to predicates, and (iii) signs referring to logical relations such as the operators of conjunction and negation. In this regard, see the reconstruction proposed by Stjernfelt (2007), p. 21. However, the abovementioned triadic typology does not appear to be exhaustive because it does not allow for the reconstruction of the particular diagrams that perform a normative function.

[25] The term 'icon' is used in a somewhat non-technical way in the theory of legal drafting. By the term 'icon,' legal design scholars usually refer to pictograms that convey their meaning through a resemblance to a physical object. In semiotics, the concept of 'icon' includes a wider typology of signs.

understanding of the term icon in the General Data Protection Regulation (GDPR). Article 12 of the GDPR presents the possibility of an iconified representation of the content of the privacy policy (according to Articles 13 and 14); moreover, recital 60 indicates the possibility of using icons to "give in an easily visible, intelligible and legible manner, a meaningful overview of the intended [data] processing." [26]

In contract drafting, companion icons[27] are simple graphic signs that are placed next to a textual element and represent part of the content graphically. For example, an icon that identifies a payment method clause can be represented by a stylized banknote.

Companion icons act as visual signals that capture the readers' attention because they graphically represent (part of) the object of the written text, and clarifying to the referent.

Including icons in every section of a document provides visual relief and provides a graphic overview for the reader.

In addition, when the same icons appear consistently across one or more documents, their meanings become familiar to the user. This ensures that recurring topics and terms are identifiable at first glance.

These icons are not autonomous, and should always be accompanied by a textual explanation or label. Icons are often highly metaphorical, as they can refer to abstract concepts and terms. However, icons can be understood without a label if they are part of a shared, standard visual lexicon.

Contract drafting is one of the legal areas that lends itself to the use of diagrams. Some legal design scholars use the expression visual images to describe the forms of contractual conceptualization or visualization that involve visual signs that are incorporated into the contract to translate certain contractual content.[28]

Similarly to written texts, diagrams must also follow precise rules in order to make the communicative act effective.

According to Amare and Manning,[29] diagrams should include clear contrasts, filter out all details except those that are relevant, and represent generalizations.

A well-formed diagram only includes the level of detail that is necessary for its purposes. As Amare and Manning stated,

> [s]ignal-processing engineers understand that an information signal at its most basic level has at least two parts: a carrier and a modulator. Modulations contrast with the basic carrier. Programmers understand that computer code has to have both zeros and ones, both "on" and "off," which have to remain distinct. Writers understand that a sentence has to have a subject and predicate (i.e., a noun and a verb). Without distinct, contrasting parts, there is no signal,

[26] Several studies have been conducted on the use of icons in the drafting of privacy policies. Some of these characterized by a multidisciplinary approach with the collaboration of graphic designers, computer scientists, and jurists. See, for example, Mondschein (2016), Efroni et al. (2019), and Rossi and Palmirani (2020).

[27] Companion icons. In: WorldCC Contract Design Pattern Library. http://contract-design.worldcc.com/companion-icons. Accessed 28 October 2022.

[28] Annola et al. (2021).

[29] Amare and Manning (2013).

> no code, no sentence, and no information. This contrastive property of information carries over in diagrams that mediate between information and perception.[30]

Visuals should not only attract the eye, but should also put viewers at ease, thus allowing them to be willing and able to inspect the visual and to make the effort to extract information from it. Diagrams should also convey a sense of visual unity or balance.[31]

Iconic representations can be used to clarify and disambiguate legal texts via intersemiotic translation. In fact, legal design theorists have identified several techniques[32] that can be traced back to this concept of iconic intersemiotic translation,[33] some of which are quite simple tools.[34]

Many visualization patterns mentioned by legal design scholars can be iconic intersemiotic legal translation instruments because they have an iconic relationship with their objects. Among the prominent examples of the possible uses of signs based on iconic relationships in the legal field are visual guides, comic contracts, and diagrams, such as timelines, flowcharts, organograms, and maps.

Images resembling physical entities, such as objects or human beings performing specific actions, can be used in intersemiotic translations to clarify parts of a legal text. This strategy is typical of comic contracts and visual guides.

Comic contracts transpose the verbal contractual text into the format of a comic. Some of the best-known comic contracts are those drafted by the South African lawyer, Robert de Roy, the founder of Creative Contracts (Pty) Ltd.

In collaboration with a professional designer, de Roy created a contract regulating the fundamental aspects of the employment relationship, such as duties, hours, salary, and methods of execution of the work performance.[35]

Among the examples of these types of iconic intersemiotic legal translations cited by legal design scholars,[36] Candy Chang's "Vendor Power" project is worth mentioning; Chang collaborated with the Center for Urban Pedagogy to create a guide for street vendors. Therefore, the Vendor Power project is mainly aimed at the more than 10,000 street vendors operating in New York,[37] who encounter serious difficulties due to linguistic and cultural barriers when undertaking street-vending activities. The project aims to inform street sellers about the rules governing this

---

[30] Amare and Manning (2013), p. 107.

[31] Ibid., p. 97.

[32] WorldCC Contract Design Pattern Library | Home. In: WorldCC Contract Design Pattern Library. http://contract-design.worldcc.com. Accessed 12 January 2022.

[33] Murray (2020).

[34] Haapio and Passera (2021).

[35] Creative Contracts | Comic Contracts everyone can understand. In: Creative Contracts. https://creative-contracts.com/. Accessed 25 October 2022.

[36] Haapio (2013).

[37] CUP: Vendor Power. http://welcometocup.org/Projects/MakingPolicyPublic/VendorPower. Accessed 6 December 2021.

particular type of trade in New York City. Street vendors are subject to quite heavy financial penalties despite belonging to low-income brackets and often being on the verge of poverty. Based on what is stated on the project's description page, the violations are sometimes due to a lack of knowledge of the current legislation. The *Vendor Power* [38] leaflet is largely composed of iconic signs; in particular, the written administrative rules are translated via images representing compliance with them. In other words, the brochure illustrates the descriptive part of the regulatory text (the description of the mandatory conduct). [39]

Another important type of iconic sign that can be employed in intersemiotic legal translations is the flowchart. Flowcharts can illustrate the phases of an activity or a procedure step by step. For example, these iconic signs can transpose the execution phases of a service into a contractual relationship. A contract can guide the contractor's choices in the different phases of the contractual relationship. A contractual relationship is not static, particularly in commercial and employment contracts. In this regard, flowcharts are tools that are aimed at supporting decision making and facilitating problem solving because they allow for the identification of how the combination of different conditions or events can lead to different results. Flowcharts are useful for translating clauses that describe processes in which different decisions lead to possible alternative outcomes and for dividing complex evaluation processes into simpler components by highlighting a series of intermediate steps. In fact, flowcharts can translate the logical structure of a procedure graphically, and can be used in the legal field to illustrate contractual documents or appendixes.[40]

A map can be an excellent tool for translating the institutional status of a specific geographic territory. Clear examples of these forms of rule visualization are maps defining a country's borders in a political treaty. [41]

The organization of a company can be visualized through an organigram which, as described by the philosopher Barry Smith, is

> a graph-theoretic structure consisting of nodes and edges. Organigrams can represent the hierarchical structure of companies as composed of the division (or business sectors) and the relations between different offices. The nodes standardly represent three sorts of entities: divisions within the organization, offices of the persons who head these divisions, and the current holders of such offices. The edges represent sub- and super-ordination relations between the entities represented by the nodes.[42]

However, the abstract concepts of "division," "office," and "organization" are presupposed in this form of representation.

[38] The leaflet is available online and is freely downloadable. Ibid.

[39] See Haapio (2013) and Berger-Walliser et al. (2017).

[40] Barton et al. (2013).

[41] As stated by Moroni and Lorini (2017), constitutive graphic rules can be found in "regulations and plans for neighbourhoods or urban districts (i.e., site plans), in regulations and plans at city-wide level (i.e., municipal master-plans, zoning ordinances and building regulations), and in plans governing land beyond the city (i.e., regional plans)".

[42] Smith (2016) *The Ontology of the Organigram* https://www.youtube.com/watch?v=bp3B2GkgaB8.

A timetable can provide a better representation of a contract clause that imposes terms, deadlines, or due dates. However, this presupposes the concepts of term and deadline.

The rules describing a procedure can be translated effectively using a cartoon or a diagram,[43] as they can follow a strategy similar to that adopted to represent technical instructions in a visual way.[44] However, in order to understand such pictures, it is necessary to have a propositional knowledge of the different phases of the procedure.

4.3 Indical Intersemiotic Legal Translation

When the target representamen is an index, the contiguity between the object and the medium of the sign determines its meaning.

According to Peirce, an index is:

> A sign, or representamen, which refers to its object not so much because of any similarity or analogy with it, nor because it is associated with general characters which that object happens to possess, as because it is in dynamical (including spatial) connection both with the individual object, on the one hand, and with the senses or memory of the person for whom it serves as a sign, on the other hand.[45]

Certain indexes are in a causal relationship with their object; for example, smoke indexes fire and a weather vane indexes wind direction, while others are conventionalized.

The latter is certainly more interesting for our purposes. Indexes that could be relevant for intersemiotic legal translation are signals, such as traffic signs and bullet points, and action triggers, such as a web page link or a button.[46]

When a companion icon is only a stylized sign without a relationship of similarity with the text content, such as a colored square or an arrow, it functions as an index. A sign that is located next to a textual component aims to draw the reader's attention to the sentence without necessarily representing its content. In addition, when the same graphic signs appear consistently across one or more documents, their meanings become familiar to the user and ensure that recurring topics and terms are identifiable at first glance. These types of signs are widely used in digital communication. According to Amare and Manning,

---

[43] Moroni and Lorini (2017), p. 327; Lorini (2016), p. 73.

[44] Szlichcinski (1980), p. 114.

[45] Peirce (1931) CP 2.305.

[46] When an index is perceived, it automatically and involuntarily captures our attention and directs it toward its object. This compelling nature of indexes is due to the strong causal relationship between the sign and what it signifies. For example, a siren is an index that attracts our attention to an emergency.

> [s]ignals cause viewers to separate mentally or to contrast whatever bits of information they point to. Action triggers require viewers to physically follow, manipulate, drag, mouse over, or click some visual display or hypertext.[47]

It is also important to note that signals and action triggers share a common property: These are physical links between concrete (material or digital) objects due to their location or physical movement toward a separate, tangible object.[48]

This means that there is a tangible relationship between the sign and what it signifies. For example, a smoke signal is an index because the smoke represents the presence of a fire. However, unlike icons, these types of signs do not have a visual resemblance to what they represent. Moreover, indexes are often used to refer to specific individuals or objects rather than to general categories.

While there may be an initial reluctance to apply indical intersemiotic translations in a legal context, recognizing the spatial component of some normative legal signs allows for the possibility of an indical intersemiotic translation despite the immaterial nature of the norms or of the legal institutions. The spatial component in some normative signs refers to the fact that some legal signs involve physical or spatial elements that are integral to their meaning. For example, road signs that indicate speed limits or parking regulations rely on their placement in a physical space to convey their intended message. This suggests that a translation can retain its original meaning and the significance of the sign even when this is expressed in a different form, such as translating a written legal document as a physical road sign.

This form of intersemiotic translation can be found in extremely simple socio-legal contexts. For example, imagine a tribe occupying a particular area of a forest. Traditionally, everyone in the tribe knows what the approximate boundaries of the tribe's territory are. However, one day, the tribal chief orders the construction of a fence that delimits the border of the tribe's territory. In this case, that enclosure is nothing more than the intersemiotic translation of the customary norm that establishes the boundaries of the tribe's territory. Clearly, the fence has a thetic dimension; the person who builds it establishes that the border is precisely in a specific place and not, for example, two centimeters behind it. However, as the fence was produced to translate a norm that may have been handed down via oral tradition into material form, it has a different semiotic code.

In fact, lawmakers make extensive use of indexes, which are indispensable tools for legal communication. Consider the border barriers installed at checkpoints, which are nothing more than the intersemiotic translation of graphic norms (authoritative maps) and the verbal norms of international treaties. These artifacts also acquire meaning by virtue of their spatial location.

The idea that it is possible to translate a legal message via an index presupposes that an index can itself be the bearer of a legal message. The investigation of deontic artifacts is relevant based on this perspective.

---

[47] Amare and Manning (2013), p. 119.

[48] Ibid., p. 125.

> A deontic artifact is an artifact–a three-dimensional material object–created in order to perform a normative function.[49]

Deontic artifacts are objects that have an indexical nature. They are semantic entities (entities with a particular meaning) that refer to a material object or to a spatial area, the referent of which is determined only in relation to the precise space-time coordinates of the object itself.

For example, as Franciszek Studnicki pointed out, a traffic sign "carries information referring to a certain section of a road—and, at the same time—indicates by its geographical position the section of the road to which that information refers."[50]

Studnicki observed that road signs only had a fully defined meaning "when the geographical positions of the sign of which they are composed are considered."[51] When examining traffic signs, their intended significance is fully realized when considered in relation to the *Origo*, as Karl Bühler termed it, which serves as the reference point within the sign's deictic field.[52]

To use Bühler's terminology, we could say that a deontic artifact usually has a "symphysical field" (in German: *symphysisches Umfeld*). [53]

In the case of normative road signs, deontic artifacts, and symphysical fields are "materially connected." For example, the symphysical field of a stop sign is the area of the road in which that sign is erected.

When used properly, an index can be an effective tool for information design, but it should only be used with deliberate, measured intent because, as with any other semantic entity, its interpretation requires the user's mental effort.

However, some forms of redundancy in road signs can result in an information overload that distracts the driver and results in dangerous situations. According to Michał Dudek,

> [t]he possibility of some signs being redundant in relation to the general function(s) of the entire road traffic law should be kept in mind during the process of planning the introduction of new signs (perhaps some new ideas are not that necessary after all) or while reconsidering the sufficiency of existing signs (perhaps some traffic signs were ultimately wrongly introduced into a given legal system).[54]

The problems related to the redundancy of road signs were highlighted in traffic engineering. From this point of view, the solutions adopted by a traffic engineer are particularly interesting and can be considered to be a form of regulation by removing

---

[49] Lorini et al. (2021), p. 190.

[50] Studnicki (1970), p. 155.

[51] Ibid., p. 155.

[52] Bühler (1934).

[53] Ibid. Eng. tr. p. 179. According to Bühler, the symphysical field is the material element—the material context—with which the artifact is materially associated. For example, "brand names are stamped on products, place-names are written on signposts and objects are 'signed' with the proper name of the owner or marker".

[54] Dudek (2022).

rules.[55] Monderman, who was the head of road safety in Friesland, the Netherlands, in 1978, removed highway measures, such as road markings and traffic signs, almost entirely in small urban centers, following a liberal approach that favored the process of the deregulation and responsibilization of drivers, which resulted in an effective reduction in casualties.[56]

However, a reduction in the number of indexes may not always be possible, as it is necessary to provide the users with information about a certain number of options. In the context of information design, it is suggested that the indexes should be organized logically to allow the users to locate the information more easily.

> The logical sequence of the index enables users to locate their personal point of interest more quickly, passing over what would otherwise be distracting, separately signaled entries, the otherwise unorganized buttons.[57]

In the context of legal design, the logical organization of indexes can be a fundamental tool.

In the contractual context, a website that allows the users to conclude an online agreement should provide the users with logically organized links to purchase additional services. The links should be organized systematically and rationally based on clear classification criteria rather than via random pop-ups that arbitrarily distract the users' attention from the main decision-making process.

As stated previously, it is important to note that a sign cannot be considered to be a standalone translation, as it only attains the status of target representamen within the context of a target artifact in relation to a source artifact. Deontic artifacts are not necessarily indical intersemiotic legal translations. Traffic lights are an example of deontic artifacts. Interestingly, according to Hart, "the red light is not merely a sign that others will stop: [drivers] look upon it as a signal for them to stop;" in this case, the red light is "a reason for stopping in conformity to rules." [58] However, traffic lights are not intersemiotic translations when they express norms independently from any source-target relationship. In this sense, the inclusion of auditory signals designed for individuals with visual impairments in conjunction with visual traffic lights can be regarded as an intersemiotic translation.

4.4 Symbolic Intersemiotic Legal Translation

In symbolic intersemiotic translations, the target representamen is a symbol; thus, it relates to its object according to a convention that determines its meaning. This type of sign determines the interpretant via a conventional relationship with the object.

[55] Lorini and Moroni (2020b), p. 4.

[56] Hamilton-Baillie (2008), p. 167.

[57] Amare and Manning (2013), p. 141.

[58] Hart (1961), p. 90. In fact, drivers may claim (from an internal point of view) that they stop when they see a red light because they are following a rule.

The relationship between sign and object is the result of a habit or a conventional rule. Words are a typical example of symbols.

According to Peirce,

> [a]ll general, or definable, Words [. . .] are certainly Symbols. That is to say, they denote the objects that they do by virtue only of there being a habit that associates their signification with them.[59]

Intersemiotic translation, as described by Jakobson, is the interpretation of a verbal sign via a non-verbal sign system. However, more recent studies on this topic have endorsed a wider definition of 'intersemiotic translation' that also includes the reverse phenomenon, namely the interpretation of a non-verbal sign by means of a verbal sign system. In symbolic intersemiotic translation, *ekphrasis*, the transposition of images into words, deserves particular attention.

According to Eco, *ekphrasis* could be considered to be a form of intersemiotic translation.[60] Since *ekphrasis* has mainly been studied with regard to the intersemiotic translations of visual artworks into text, it has essentially been defined as a specific literary genre. As Eco pointed out:

> As a matter of fact, even today, many poems and stories begin life as the description of a visual work.[61]

Many visual works of art have come down to us only through their transpositions into words. Art studies are one of the areas in which *ekphrasis* is applied most frequently. However, the practice of *ekphrasis* has limitations; according to Eco:

> The practice of ekphrasis makes it possible to describe an image in words, but no ekphrasis of Raphael's Wedding of the Virgin could convey the sense of perspective perceived by the viewer, the flowing lines that manifest the position of the bodies, or the tenuous harmony of the colors.[62]

The phenomenon of *ekphrasis* is relevant to legal communication, and raises questions pertaining to the translatability of normative images into words.

Some scholars have highlighted the limitations of *ekphrasis* in legal studies. For example, according to Boehme-Neßler, "images can transmit the information which cannot be reproduced in the text."[63] Moreover, as Lorini and Moroni stated:

> A zoning map can be transformed into a detailed verbal description of the boundaries of the various zones, but it would be highly impractical and very expensive. Moreover, thus lost would be the overview of how the various norms interact in spatial terms; that is, the "adjacency" dimension characteristic of (normative) maps. In the case of road signs, the linguistic form would make it more difficult, if not impossible, to perceive the norm while driving.[64]

---

[59] Peirce (1931). CP 4.544.

[60] Eco (2003a), p. 110.

[61] Ibid., p. 110.

[62] Eco (2001), p. 97.

[63] Boehme-Neßler (2011), p. 74.

[64] Lorini and Moroni (2020a), p. 68.

Lorini and Moroni[65] emphasized that urban planning actively employed graphic rules. More precisely, the production of rules takes place through the creation of maps and drawings in urban planning; illustrative reports flank the plans and actively translate intersemiotically what the maps present. However, something is still lost in translation, regardless of whether this is due to pragmatic or other reasons.

John Searle supported the principle of expressibility; that is, whatever can be meant can be said.[66] Surely the intersemiotic relationships that connect verbal texts and non-verbal representamen that are composed of images, for example, can be extremely difficult to reconstruct.

However, the fact that a norm can be expressed linguistically does not mean

(i) that it is intrinsically a linguistic entity,
(ii) that nothing is lost in translation,[67] and
(iii) that words are always the most efficient semiotic resource in translations.

4.5 Strategies for Intersemiotic Legal Translation

In the previous paragraphs, we examined the possible links between the target representamen and its object, and applied Peirce's distinction among icons, symbols, and indexes to the classification of intersemiotic legal translations.

A different issue arises when considering not only the relationship between the sign and its object, but also the medium selected by the translator for the creation of the target representamen. We will focus on four possibilities in particular:

(i) estures,
(ii) two-dimensional representations (such as drawings or pictures),
(iii) material artifacts (such as physical objects), and
(iv) digital artifacts.

Every translation presupposes implicit assumptions about what is important to show, as well as how best we can show it.

While it is not difficult to represent a physical object or a brute fact with a non-verbal sign, it must be admitted that translating deontic concepts without the aid of words poses a number of difficulties.

Since an intersemiotic legal translation is primarily a translation of norms and involves deontic concepts, one may consider this to be an objection to the concept of intersemiotic legal translation itself. As a result, it could be argued that any form of

[65] Moroni and Lorini (2017).

[66] Searle (1969), pp. 19–21. John Searle (2020), p. 57 attributed a semantic supremacy to verbal language and criticized semiotics harshly for not taking this primacy into consideration. This primacy is mainly derived from the fact that "the expressive power of language vastly exceeds that of signs in general. This is because language produces sentences and these sentences represent entire conditions of satisfaction, and are subject to compositionality and generativity."

[67] Lorini and Moroni (2020a), p. 68.

legal translation can only be interlingual, and can only occur within the context of linguistic semiotic systems.[68] However, specific strategies can be used to overcome the mentioned difficulties.

Gestures can exhibit distinct patterns of action while prompting corresponding or similar behavior. These gestures can be accompanied by a straightforward expression explicitly emphasizing the obligatory nature of the behavior, as mentioned previously (Sect. 2.2.1), such as saying "do as I do." The normative aspect of behavior can also be subtly concealed behind a descriptive expression. An illustrative example in this regard could be when a father gracefully removes his hat within a church setting and instructs his son, "Gentlemen behave in this manner." In this particular case, the father likely intends to convey the following message to his son: "Young man, comport yourself as a gentleman in this manner."

These modes of normative representation tap into the innate mechanisms of imitation. They not only describe a pattern of action, but also guide the recipient's actions. The philosopher Ruth Millikan referred to such representations as "pushmi-pullyu representations."[69] In Millikan's words, pushmi-pullyu representations "mediate between perception and action [. . .] they at the same time tell what the case is with some part of the world and direct what to do about it."[70] According to Millikan, *pushmi-pullyu representations* are neither reducible to descriptive representations nor to directives, but are a different and more primitive form of normative communication.

Various animals use pushmi-pullyu representations for communicating with members of the same species. In this regard, possible channels of pushmi-pullyu representation include the singing of birds, the thumping of rabbits, and the dancing of bees. Honeybees employ a behavioral pattern called the waggle dance to convey precise information regarding the location of food sources to other bees within the hive.

Pushmi-pullyu representations also influence our understanding of the behavior we must enact in certain social contexts. An example of this type of normative representation that we encounter in our daily lives is the safety demonstration performed by flight attendants. The flight attendants' simple gestures are intended to communicate a prescription to the passengers (for example, passengers must fast their seatbelts), while simultaneously demonstrating how to do so. These pushmi-pullyu representations are actually an intersemiotic translation of the flight attendants' verbal instructions.

Several applications of this strategy can be made. These applications also concern bidimensional artifacts, such as drawings. For example, the illustrations that appear in contractual documents and represent methods for executing certain tasks to fulfill contractual obligations via drawings also have a descriptive and a prescriptive nature; the same applies to the videos and cartoons that translate how passengers

[68] Tuzet (2015).

[69] Millikan (2006), p. 87.

[70] Ibid.

should behave in a public place intersemiotically, such as on public transportation. These are intersemiotic translations in which different visual channels, such as gestures, videos, or drawings, are used.

Drawings and other forms of two-dimensional graphic representation play a crucial role in establishing and communicating instructions for architectural projects, as well as for building and assembling objects. In the fields of architecture and industry, the use of drawings, with their syntactic and semantic characteristics, allows for precise communication that surpasses the expressive capabilities of verbal language, both in terms of content and of interpretation.[71] Drawings are also essential for communicating how to create architectural works or how to manufacture and assemble various items accurately. Drawings provide a level of detail and clarity that verbal language alone may not achieve.

Drawings are frequently used for regulatory purposes in various contexts. Examples of regulatory drawings include road signs, maps displaying regulatory plans, and signals found in public places, stations, ports, and airports.

Drawings can acquire a normative meaning or fulfill a normative role through customary practices, established conventions, or legally formalized models. Models of regulatory drawings can be understood as meta-norms that define the types of single occurrences of the standards depicted. For example, the metarules depicted in the *Vienna Convention on Road Signs and Signals* (1968) are adopted across most of the world as criteria for designing the graphic norms of road signs. The expression graphic norms indicates drawings that are characterized by a normative function. They are not simply signs that evoke or refer to other rules expressed via words, as graphic norms express prescriptions directly.[72]

Drafting the graphic norms can be an integral part of a legislative process. For example, in Italy, identifying the designers who draw the urban planning maps is an integral part of the procedure that leads to the approval of the graphic norms contained therein.[73]

A classic way of translating verbal rules consists of showing the *negative result of deviant behavior*. As in pushmi-pullyu representations, a descriptive element emerges in this method of representation. However, it should be noted that this strategy differs from pushmi-pullyu representation because it emphasizes the consequences of the deviant behavior more than it does the regulated behavior. In normative pictures, the negative consequences can originate directly from deviant behavior as *ontic consequences* or from rules as *deontic consequences*; for example, social or formal sanctions. An example of this strategy is the forced removal sign (Fig. 4.3). The sign highlights the negative consequences of norm violation by showing the car being towed away. It visually represents the undesired outcome of disregarding the rules, aiming to discourage people from ignoring the regulations and emphasizing the importance of compliance to avoid inconvenient situations or

[71] Maynard (2005).

[72] Lorini and Moroni (2020a).

[73] Legge 17 agosto 1942, n. 1150, art. 8.

Fig. 4.3 The sign displays a rule that imposes that parking of the vehicles in unauthorised locations will lead to their forcible removal. Author rendering

additional costs associated with vehicle removal. Another example of this strategy is the image showing the negative consequences of using public transport without a ticket; that is, a drawing representing a ticket controller who fines a transgressor can translate the following legal regulation that is expressed in words:

> Passengers can use buses only if provided with regular tickets or travelcards [. . .] Traveling by bus with no proper or irregular ticket involves the application of fines which the Regional Law regulates.[74]

This strategy also characterizes intersemiotic translations concerning rules in which the binding force is based on the threat of the negative consequences of rule violation rather than on a formal sanction to a greater extent.

---

[74] ATC La Spezia. Tickets and regulations. In: ATC Esercizio. https://www.atcesercizio.it/en/fines/. Accessed 20 October 2022.

For example, a warning picture can represent the physical damage (or events that can cause physical injuries) due to the deviant behavior. A classic example of this type of normative picture is a danger sign. Some intersemiotic representations that aim to persuade the addressee to avoid a particular behavior without expressing a real obligation follow the same strategy.

Another strategy consists of *making use of symbolic representations*. This is one of the most traditional ways of translating a verbal normative message using signs that belong to a different semiotic system. A typical example is an icon in a circle-backslash symbol. The elements involved in these forms of intersemiotic legal translation are usually partly conventional and partially pictorial. More precisely, these representations consist of a predicate (a deontic operator, such as forbidden or obligatory) and an argument of that predicate, which enables the identification of what is forbidden. [75] In Hare's lexicon, [76] on one hand, the icon is a phrastic; that is, it is a reference to actual or possible states of affairs, such as a running man. On the other hand, a neustic also determines the sign's (normative) modality; for example, a circle-backslash symbol. The neustic cannot be expressed explicitly via icons due to its referential opacity. [77]

It must be admitted that there are some limitations to the graphic representation of a rule, particularly of a legal rule, because it is impossible to produce a direct representation of elements of social reality, such obligations or prime ministers. Therefore, it is not infrequent for the target artifact in intersemiotic legal translation to present textual elements and to combine the potential of verbal language with that of visual language. Intersemiotic translations from verbal to visual language can be of three types:

(1) *Total translation*. The drawing fully translates the rule. The entire translation is monomodal. The translator uses a single semiotic system that is different from the source text. We can summarize this form of translation as follows:

$$\text{Text} \rightarrow \text{Image}$$

(2) *Partial translation*. The drawing translates part of the source text. Its normative meaning can only be interpreted correctly in combination with verbal signs. It is a multimodal translation, since the product of the translation activity uses different semiotic systems. We can schematize this form of translation as follows:

---

[75] Lorini and Loddo (2017). See also Maynard (2017, p. 335).

[76] Hare (1952), pp. 17–28.

[77] The hybrid nature of these pictures (partly symbolic and partly iconic) has led some scholars of informal logic to consider them as a type of "linguistic use of a visual form". These scholars (e.g. Worth 1981; Fleming 1996; Johnson 2003; Groarke 1996) have aimed to describe visual communications as being entirely subordinate to verbal language. Their position presupposes a type of reductionism. In fact, they reduce the concept of the picture to the idea of the icon and exclude the other signs from the realm of pictures. In doing so, they overlook an essential aspect of visual communication: Visual languages possess their own grammars.

$$\text{Text} \rightarrow \text{Image} + \text{Text}$$

(3) *Intersemiotic redundancy*. This is a form of multimodal translation *in praesentia*. The source text and its intersemiotic transposition appear simultaneously in the translated document. Both the source text and its intersemiotic transposition express the same meaning, albeit via different semiotic tools. We can summarize this form of translation as follows:

$$\text{Text} \rightarrow \text{Image} \approx \text{Text}$$

An intersemiotic translation of norms, accomplished through drawings, presupposes both the ability of the graphic language to express normative meanings and that of having a regulative function. However, the translatant does not necessarily have the same function as the translated text. Drawings can also translate descriptive statements of norms. An interesting example is exemplified by normative pictograms, which constitute one of the most well-known symbols of the community of Christiania: Christiania common law. Christiania is a self-proclaimed autonomous neighbourhood located in the centre of Copenhagen.[78] Christiania's normative pictograms are intersemiotic translations of normative statements in English and in Danish that have a descriptive function. In fact, these statements describe the rules that were in force within the community prior to their graphic representation; therefore, the binding force of these rules is independent of their graphic representation. The norms of Christiania were graphically represented based on the decisions taken by the community gathered in a common assembly [Fællesmøde]. In particular, Christiania's common assembly commissioned a local artist, Anna Tengberg, to graphically represent the provisions of the Christiania constitution. Subsequently, the legal artwork was disseminated via publication in the local newspaper, as well as through the use of posters and stickers that were strategically placed throughout Christiania.

In addition to two-dimensional representations, *material artifacts* play a significant role as possible tools for normative communication and intersemiotic legal translations. We previously mentioned deontic artifacts, which are artifacts[79] that are intentionally designed and constructed to regulate human behavior according to norms and rules. Due to their indical nature (Sect. 4.3), deontic artifacts have a distinct deontic meaning, which is closely linked to the specific location in which they are positioned.[80] In other words, they assume a specific normative meaning due to their placement on a material support that is located in a specific spatial area. A red

[78] For a more detailed analysis of Christiania common law, see Lorini and Loddo (2017).

[79] Dipert (1995), p. 117. According to Dipert, artifacts are material objects that not only perform specific functions but also provide the observer with information about themselves and their function. In Dipert's words, artifacts "manifest their nature as tools and are, in this respect, inherently communicative."

[80] Lorini et al. (2021).

flag placed on a buoy or pole in the middle of the sea is a deontic artifact, and can translate the phrase "No swimming." In another context, a red flag can represent a symbol of political ideology. An important peculiarity of deontic artifacts is that they pose norms that can be violated.

Material artifacts are not the only type of artifact that can perform a regulatory function. In particular circumstances, even software can assume this function. In this regard, we can talk about digital (regulative) artifacts. Some authors have used the expression *lex informatica*[81] to refer to the "substantive inalienable rules"[82] deriving from the architectural choices of a developer.[83] In reality, the developer does not set real rules, but translates rules into structures through computer codes, which impose models of behavior, protect rights, and limit conduct. In particular, a digital architecture can perform a regulatory function that was originally performed by a legal rule. An example of this form of translation, as highlighted by Lawrence Lessig, may concern the rules aimed at protecting property in cyberspace. In this regard, according to Lessig, two types of protection are possible:

> One is the traditional protection of the law—the law defines a space where others should not enter and punishes people who enter nonetheless. The other protection is a fence, a technological device (a bit of code) that (among other things) blocks the unwanted from entering.[84]

The "bit of code" that Lessig discussed is nothing more than a digital regulatory artifact. Furthermore, it is an intersemiotic translation of norms to the extent that the artifact performs a regulatory function borrowed from legal norms.

Regulatory deontic artifacts combine a material dimension with an immaterial-symbolic dimension. The connection between the two dimensions occurs through high-level and low-level programming languages. Digital deontic artifacts are only software or parts of software that can only exercise their normative function through the material support of hardware which, when connected to an output device (for example, a computer monitor), allows for the communication of the regulatory content to the addressee.

Digital deontic artifacts can convey normative content relating to material reality and normative content relating to digital reality; for example, they can provide indications about what is allowed or forbidden on particular areas of a digital platform, or they can allow for the reading and concluding of electronic contracts.

We can also use a digital artifact to translate a highway code. For example, some software can provide directions to the user while driving, and can provide information about the regulations in force along the indicated route, such as speed limits or temporary road interruptions. The information is conveyed through graphic icons displayed on the device's screen, auditory signals, or voice commands directed

---

[81] Chapter 5 of this book will provide a more detailed examination of this topic.

[82] Reidenberg (1998), p. 572.

[83] Ibid.

[84] Lessig (2006), p. 235.

toward the user, and tactile feedback such as vibrations on the steering wheel when crossing the center line.

On-going advancements are being made in the development of driving assistance systems. These devices are able to automatically convert the regulatory information into instructions addressed not to the user, but to the electronic system that controls the vehicle, thus determining an automatic fulfillment of the rule.[85] Examples of such regulatory artifacts include automated speed limit regulators.[86]

4.6 The Typology of Rules in Intersemiotic Translations

As mentioned previously, the structure of the target representamen in an intersemiotic legal translation does not necessarily correspond to the structure of the rule that is being represented.

It is essential to emphasize that the semiotic dimension does not coincide with the normative dimension to comprehend the mechanisms underpinning intersemiotic translations.

To support this last statement, we can consider an intersemiotic legal translation from words to pictures, and we can compare the distinction between rules and metarules (as adopted in legal studies) to the distinction between pictures and metapictures (typical of visual studies). It is well known that a metarule is a rule that affects the content, form, mode of application of another rule. On one hand, a metarule is a rule that refers to other rules; on the other hand, metapictures are pictures that "refer to themselves or other pictures."[87]

There can also be normative metapictures, namely normative pictures, which refer to other pictures.[88] The *Vienna Convention on Road Signs and Signals*' graphical representations of traffic signs can be considered to be metapictures because they refer to other pictures; specifically, to the various shapes of traffic signs. In addition, these metapictures serve as metarules because they refer to the regulations that govern traffic and are enforced through the use of traffic signs. In essence, the traffic signs depicted in the *Vienna Convention on Road Signs and Signals* determine how traffic rules are communicated visually.

However, it is important to note that normative metapictures do not necessarily express metarules in the same way that legal terminology differentiates between rules and metarules. Therefore, it is important to avoid confusing the distinction between pictures and metapictures with the differentiation between rules and metarules, which is commonly used in legal discourse. An example of a metapicture

---

[85] Caprino (2022).

[86] Questo ulteriore sviluppo ci porta a prendere in esame una peculiare forma di traduzione intersemiotica, caratterizzata da un processo di risemiotizzazione (See Sect. 5.2.3).

[87] Mitchell (1994), p. 35.

[88] Loddo (2020).

is a "no graffiti" sign that incorporates the image of a hand drawing graffiti inside of a circle-backslash symbol. This metapicture alludes to other pictures (graffiti) but does not overtly convey a metarule. Of note, the prohibition of graffiti could also be represented by a conventional picture instead of by a metapicture by portraying a spray can (a tool associated with graffiti) within a circle-backslash symbol.[89]

The process of intersemiotic translation poses specific challenges when considering constitutive rules because not all rules are solely prescriptive or regulatory. As Searle pointed out, "Some rules do not merely regulate; they also create the very possibility of certain activities" [90]: For this reason, Searle called them "constitutive rules." Constitutive rules have immense significance in our society because they are foundational elements of social reality. They establish the necessary conditions for the existence of institutional facts, such as prime ministers, governments, parliaments, and elections. By contrast, prescriptive rules govern pre-existing behaviors, such smoking, eating, or running; for example, "no smoking" represents a prescriptive rule.

Let us now address the following questions:

1. Does the intersemiotic translation of a rule need to be aligned with the typology of the rule being represented?
2. Is it essential for the intersemiotic translation of a rule to correspond to its represented rule type?

Using a combination of icons and symbols as a representation strategy can translate regulatory rules effectively, but it encounters limitations when attempting to present constitutive rules visually. Specifically, it becomes challenging to find visual representations resembling tangible objects that can depict the actions created and governed by constitutive rules, such as voting, buying, or selling.

This limitation arises because, while regulatory rules mainly exhibit referential opacity in their neustic aspect (often implicit or represented by conventional signs), the actions regulated by constitutive rules display complete referential opacity.

An institutional fact can be represented by associating it with the corresponding brute fact that is typically associated with it in a specific social context. For example, depicting a hand placing a ballot in a ballot box can indirectly represent the act of

---

[89]Loddo (2020), pp. 568–569.

[90]Searle (1995), p. 146. Searle (1995, 2010) claimed that all constitutive rules had the form "x count as y in the contest c", where x is the brute fact and y is the institutional fact. In fact, this logical formalisation is quite naïve and has been challenged by many authors. The category of constitutive rules is somewhat vague and includes many subcategories. Some authors have supported the theory that it is possible to classify the constitutive rules by establishing if the rule is or poses the condition (necessary, sufficient, or necessary and sufficient) of what the rule regulates. See Azzoni (1988), Conte (1997), and Lorini (2017). For a critical analysis of constitutive rules, see Żełaniec (2013) and Roversi (2021). An alternative distinction was proposed by MacCormick (2008), who classified the rules according to their functions and differentiated among "institutive, consequential, and terminative rules."

voting, which serves as a prominent example of an institutional fact. This approach can also indirectly represent the rule underlying the institutional fact.[91]

4.7 Conclusion

In this chapter, we identified three types of intersemiotic translation based on the types of relationships that the target can have with its object.

In this sense, it is possible to differentiate among iconic, indical, and symbolic intersemiotic translation. We also highlighted how these translations can be used in the legal field.

It should be clarified that this classification is a simplification; an intersemiotic legal translation is rarely purely iconic, indical, or symbolic. Intersemiotic translations can combine icons, indices, and symbols. These strategies are particularly suitable for translating rules that regulate (prohibit or make mandatory) acts consisting of specific brute facts that existed prior to the rule and can be represented via an icon, such as running, smoking, walking, picking flowers, and drawing graffiti.

Peirce's theory of signs[92] is important when we examine forms of intersemiotic translation that combine different types of signs, such as symbolic and iconic signs. As Amare and Manning stated:

> Iconic interpretation by similarity and symbolic interpretation by code require different kinds of "cultural context." Peircean analysis allows us to keep those diverse types of "context" distinct, even as they are mixed together in one visual.[93]

Moreover, as mentioned previously, figurative representations have several limitations. In fact, icons can take the form of specific objects (a cigarette, a spray can, or a masculine or feminine human figure in a specific position), but they usually symbolize categories of objects and, particularly in the case of normative pictures, categories of actions.[94]

The meaning of an easily understandable normative picture, such as a graphic composed of a cigarette in a circle-backslash symbol, can be extrapolated through an interpretative process that is constructed based on the background knowledge of its observers and the specific situation. In fact, the graphic composed of a cigarette in a circle-backslash symbol expresses the norm "no smoking," which prohibits the smoking of cigarettes, as well as of cigars and pipes. Moreover, the "no smoking" sign does not prohibit one from having cigarettes, cigars, or pipes in one's pocket. Nonetheless, we can find normative signs that prohibit carrying specific objects in

[91] For constitutive graphic rules, see Lorini and Moroni (2017, 2020a).

[92] Peirce (1931). CP.

[93] Amare and Manning (2013), p. 198.

[94] Tijus et al. (2007).

hand luggage, with similar morphologies to the "no smoking" signs, in every airport. In a certain sense, the ambiguity of an icon is the reverse of the ambiguity of a word; whereas a word expresses a concept that is often too general, a picture, on the contrary, may be too specific. In the first case, the difficulty is understanding the types of acts or objects that should be included in the category. The classic example is the written rule "no vehicles allowed": "Plainly this forbids an automobile, but what about bicycles, roller skates, toy automobiles?"[95] In the case of normative pictures, the first difficulty that the observer should overcome is to infer the category from the picture (from particular to general). For example, a 'no vehicle sign' could be a picture of a car in a circle-backslash symbol. The observer could have some difficulty understanding whether the normative picture, and thus the prohibition, refers only to cars or also to other vehicles.[96] The background against which the normative pictures operate has a significant impact on their interpretation.

To translate a rule accurately, the translator must consider how and where the hypothetical recipient will perceive the normative message and what the rule aims to regulate.

As mentioned previously, the intersemiotic translation of institutional facts is particularly problematic. However, the translator could exploit a connection between a physical object and the institutional fact rooted in mainstream thinking. For example, in a contract, the iconic representation of a judge gavel can be used to illustrate the clause that identifies the court competent in the event of a dispute.

Legal designers should consider the typology of the rule that they aims to represent in graphic form. The designers' choices are essential from practical and epistemological perspectives.

References

Amare N, Manning A (2013) A unified theory of information design: visuals, text and ethics. Routledge, London

Annola V, Haapio H, Koskela M (2021) Interpreting images in contracts. In: Corrales Compagnucci M, Haapio H, Fenwick M (eds) Research handbook on contract design. Elgar, Northampton

Azzoni G (1988) Il concetto di condizione nella tipologia delle regole. CEDAM, Padova

Barton T, Berger-Walliser G, Haapio H (2013) Visualization: seeing contracts for what they are, and what they could become. Journal of Law, Business, & Ethics 19:47–64

Berger-Walliser G, Barton TD, Haapio H (2017) A collaborative and creative process: from visualization to legal design. American Business Law Journal 54:347–392. https://doi.org/10.1111/ablj.12101

Bobbio N (1993) Teoria generale del diritto. Giappichelli, Torino

Boehme-Neßler V (2011) Pictorial Law. Modern law and the power of pictures. Springer, Berlin

Bühler K (1934) Sprachtheorie. Die Darstellungsfunktion der Sprache, Fischer, Jena

[95] Hart (1958), p. 607.

[96] .Ibid.

Caprino M (2022) Le auto del futuro? Rispettano da sole i limiti di velocità ed "evitano" i colpi di sonno. In: Il Sole 24 ORE. https://www.ilsole24ore.com/art/auto-tutti-modelli-nuovi-rispetteranno-soli-limiti-velocita-e-vigileranno-contro-colpi-sonno-AEni2kAB. Accessed 12 Oct 2022

Conte AG (1997) Eidetic-constitutive rules. In: Jori M (ed) Pintore A. Law and language. The Italian analytical school. Deborah Charles Publications, Liverpool

Di Lucia P, Passerini Glazel L (2022) Towards a Sigmatics of the word 'norm': an ontological turn in the semiotics of the normative. International Journal for the Semiotics of Law 36: 83-104. https://doi.org/10.1007/s11196-022-09921-6

Dipert RR (1995) Some issues in the theory of artifacts: defining 'artifact' and related notions. The Monist 78:119–135

Dudek M (2022) Redundancies of traffic signs: an exploratory study. Semiotica 247:283–317. https://doi.org/10.1515/sem-2020-0128

Eco U (1999) Kant and the platypus. Essays on language and cognition. Harcourt, San Diego

Eco U (2000) Traduzione e interpretazione. Quaderni di studi semiotici 85/86/87:55–100

Eco U (2001) Experiences in translation. University of Toronto Press, Toronto

Eco U (2003a) Mouse or Rat? Translation as negotiation. Phoenix, London

Eco U (2003b) Dire quasi la stessa cosa. Esperienze di traduzione, Bompiani, Milano

Efroni Z, Metzger J, Mischau L, Schirmbeck M (2019) Privacy icons: a risk-based approach to visualisation of data processing. European Data Protection Law Review (EDPL) 5:352–366

Haapio H (2013) Contract clarity and usability through visualization. In: Marchese FT, Banassi E (eds) Knowledge visualization currents. From text to art to culture. Springer, London, pp 63–84

Haapio H, Passera S (2021) Contracts as interfaces: exploring visual representation patterns in contract design. In: Katz DM, Dolin R, Bommarito M (eds) Legal informatics. Cambridge University Press, Cambridge, pp 213–238

Hamilton-Baillie B (2008) Shared space: reconciling people, places and traffic. Built Environment 34:161–181. https://doi.org/10.2148/benv.34.2.161

Hare RM (1952) The language of morals. Clarendon Press, Oxford

Hart HLA (1958) Positivism and the separation of law and morals. Harvard Law Review 71:593. https://doi.org/10.2307/1338225

Hart HLA (1961) The concept of law. 3rd edn., 2012. Oxford University Press, Oxford

Jakobson R (1959) On linguistic aspects of translation. In: Brower RA (ed) On translation. MIT Press, London, pp 232–239

Krampen M (1983) Icons of the road. Semiotica 43:1–204

Lessig L (2006) Code. Version 2.0. Basic Books, New York

Loddo OG (2017) Drawing an Unwritten Common Law. Archiv für Rechts- und Sozialphilosophie 103:101–116

Loddo OG (2020) The background of normative pictures. Archiv für Rechts- und Sozialphilosophie 106:563. https://doi.org/10.25162/arsp-2020-0023

Lorini G (2016) Il senso e la norma. Giappichelli, Torino

Lorini G (2017) Anankastico in deontica. LED, Milano

Lorini G, Loddo OG (2017) Thinking of norms spatially. Rechtstheorie 48:197–211

Lorini G, Loddo OG (2022) Legal objects: essence and existence. In: The new yearbook for phenomenology and phenomenological philosophy, vol XIX. Routledge, London, pp 39–54

Lorini G, Moroni S (2020a) How to make norms with drawings: an investigation of normativity beyond the realm of words. Semiotica 233:55–76. https://doi.org/10.1515/sem-2018-0062

Lorini G, Moroni S (2020b) Ruling without rules. Regulation beyond normativity. Global Jurist 20: 1–11. https://doi.org/10.1515/gj-2019-0051

Lorini G, Moroni S, Loddo OG (2021) Deontic artifacts. Investigating the normativity of objects. Philosophical Explorations 24:185–203. https://doi.org/10.1080/13869795.2021.1908584

MacCormick N (2008) Institutions of Law: an essay in legal theory. Oxford University Press, Oxford

Maynard P (2005) Drawing distinctions: the varieties of graphic expression. Cornell University Press, Ithaca
Maynard P (2017) Drawn norms: the example of traffic signs. In: Lecis P, Lorini G, Busacchi V et al (eds) Truth, image, normativity. Quodlibet, Macerata, pp 327–352
Millikan RG (2006) Language: a biological model. Clarendon Press, Oxford
Mitchell WJT (1994) Picture theory essays on verbal and visual representation. The University of Chicago Press, Chicago
Mondschein CF (2016) Some iconoclastic thoughts on the effectiveness of simplified notices and icons for informing individuals as proposed in Article 12(1) and (7) GDPR. European Data Protection Law Review (EDPL) 2:507–520. https://doi.org/10.21552/EDPL/2016/4/9
Moroni S, Lorini G (2017) Graphic rules in planning: a critical exploration of normative drawings starting from zoning maps and form-based codes. Plan Theory 16:318–338. https://doi.org/10.1177/1473095216656389
Murray MD (2020) Diagrammatics and the proactive visualization of legal information. University of Arkansas at Little Rock Law Review 43:1–50
Peirce CS (1931) The collected papers of Charles Sanders Peirce. Harvard University Press, Cambridge
Plaza J (1987) Tradução intersemiótica. Perspectiva, São Paulo
Polidoro P (2015) Umberto Eco and the problem of Iconism. Semiotica 206:129–160. https://doi.org/10.1515/sem-2015-0020
Queiroz J, Aguiar D (2015) C. S. Peirce and Intersemiotic Translation. In: Trifonas P (ed) International Handbook of Semiotics. Springer, Dordrecht, pp 201–215
Reidenberg JR (1998) Lex informatica: the formulation of information policy rules through technology. Texas Law Review 76:553–594
Rossi A, Palmirani M (2020) Can visual design provide legal transparency? The challenges for successful implementation of icons for data protection. Design Issues 36:82–96. https://doi.org/10.1162/desi_a_00605
Roversi C (2021) In defence of constitutive rules. Synthese 199: 14349–14370. https://doi.org/10.1007/s11229-021-03424-w
Searle JR (1969) Speech acts: an essay in the philosophy of language. Cambridge University Press, Cambridge
Searle JR (1995) The construction of social reality. Allen Lane, London
Searle JR (2010) Making the social world. The structure of human civilization. Oxford University Press, Oxford
Searle JR (2020) Semiotics as a theory of representation. Teoria e critica della regolazione sociale 1:49–57. https://doi.org/10.7413/19705476017
Stjernfelt F (2007) Diagrammatology: an investigation on the borderlines of phenomenology, ontology, and semiotics. Springer, Dordrecht
Studnicki F (1970) Traffic signs. Semiotica 2:151–172
Szlichcinski KP (1980) The syntax of pictorial instructions. In: Kolers PA, Wrolstad ME, Bouma H (eds) Processing of visible language. Springer, Boston, pp 113–124
Tijus C, Barcenilla J, Lavalette Cambon de B, Meunier J-G (2007) The design, understanding and usage of pictograms. In: Alamargot DJ, Terrier P, Cellier J-M (eds) Written documents in the workplace. Brill, pp 17–31
Tuzet G (2015) Contro le immagini. In: Faralli C, Gigliotti V, Heritier P, Mittica MP (eds) Il diritto tra testo e immagine. Rappresentazione ed evoluzione delle fonti. Mimesis, Milano-Udine, pp 175–188
Watson A (1993) Legal transplants. An approach to comparative law, 2nd edn. University of Georgia Press, Athens
Żełaniec W (2013) Create to Rule: Studies on Constitutive Rules. LED, Milano

Chapter 5
Intersemiotic Legal Translation as a Process

5.1 Introduction

The term 'intersemiotic translation' has taken on a broader meaning than Jakobson originally intended when he first introduced it. As mentioned previously, Queiroz and Aguiar correctly pointed out that intersemiotic translation "is not restricted to the interpretation of verbal signs."[1]

Semioticians and theorists of translation have engaged in active debate about the concept of intersemiotic translation. When considering the debate about intersemiotic translation, we can see that there are at least four different conceptions of intersemiotic translation that are worth mentioning. As a result of the four perspectives examined, intersemiotic translation has been described as an adaptation, an illustration, a resemiotization, and a transactional process, respectively. Of note, each conception focuses on a specific aspect of intersemiotic translation that a legal design technique can exemplify. There is no inherent incompatibility among the different concepts of intersemiotic translations that we have examined; instead, they focus on different forms of intersemiotic translation or on different aspects of the same phenomenon.

It is important to note that the concepts of intersemiotic translation as adaptation, illustration, and resemiotization emphasize the relationship between the substratum of the source representamen and that of the target representamen.

The process of illustration creates an artifact that includes the target representamen. In this case, the source and the target representamen usually appear in the same document and share the same material substratum. The addressee can perceive both simultaneously. The process of adaptation produces an artifact that is autonomous from the target representamen.

The concept of intersemiotic translation as resemiotization focuses on the process of intersemiotic translation that can give rise to a target artifact. While maintaining a

[1] Queiroz and Aguiar (2015), p. 201.

O. G. Loddo, *Intersemiotic Legal Translation*, Law and Visual Jurisprudence 11,
https://doi.org/10.1007/978-3-031-44184-4_5

genetic and functional connection to the source, this target artifact acquires different semiotic properties via a process of reification. This semiotic transformation can also result in the loss of some semiotic characteristics in the target representamen. In the case of the translation of a normative text, resemiotization can lead to the loss of the deontic dimension while retaining the regulatory function of the source representamen.

If we consider a concept that *highlights specific aspects of intersemiotic translation* that can simultaneously characterize all the forms of intersemiotic translation instead, we will see that intersemiotic translation can be considered to be a transactional process. The concept of intersemiotic translation as a transactional process highlights the potential of intersemiotic translation as a tool for intercultural interaction.

We do not specifically endorse any of these conceptions; in our opinion, both illustration adaptation and resemiotization are forms of intersemiotic translation. Moreover, any intersemiotic translation can be a transactional process.

Although all the concepts of intersemiotic translation originated from the same conceptual framework provided by Jakobson, [2] they can be used as theoretical tools to clarify intersemiotic translation in several legal contexts. We will attempt to clarify this consideration through a more precise analysis of the four different conceptions of intersemiotic translation accompanied by examples taken from legal design techniques.

5.2 Producing a Target Representamen in Intersemiotic Translation

As with any form of communication, the product of an intersemiotic translation necessarily has a physical dimension; this material substrate could be a computer and its output devices, a group of sheets of paper, or a material artifact.

In some cases, the substratum of the intersemiotic translation is autonomous from the source; in this case, the target representamen acquires meaning for the recipient regardless of whether the source is accessible. In this regard, we can consider the target representamen to be an adaptation of the source representamen. As Umberto Eco stated,

> [t]he commonest cases concern the adaptation of a novel for a film, or occasionally for a theatrical piece, but there is also the adaptation of a fairy tale for a ballet, or for example, of a poem into a musical composition, of a musical composition into a painting or vice versa.[3]

In other cases, the translator creates a target representamen that includes the source representamen in the same substratum. An illustration is a form of intersemiotic

[2] Jakobson (1959).

[3] Eco (2003a), p. 158. See also Dusi (2015), p. 184.

translation *in praesentia*, in which the translator selects some parts of the source representamen and translates them intersemiotically.

5.2.1 Intersemiotic Translation as Adaptation

According to Eco, intersemiotic translation cannot be considered anything other than adaptation. The process of intersemiotic translation involves a significant transformation of the original text, often leading to a clear exposition of implicit meanings.[4]

Following Linda Hutcheon's definition, adaptations are

> [o]penly acknowledged and extended reworkings of particular other texts. [5]

A fundamental characteristic of adaptation is the autonomy from the original text. In the adaptation process, the translator not only uses a different communication channel from that used in the source representamen, but also effects profound changes with regard to the source representamen. In some way, the translator uses the source to create something new. Umberto Eco[6] mentioned many cases of adaptations that represent original artworks, such as Visconti's film *La morte a Venezia* [*Death in Venice*], which is a work that is distinct from Mann's novel. In Eco's words:

> If we were not told that that film intended to "translate" that novel, we would leave the room admiring and satisfied by those highly original inventions.[7]

The transposition of a verbal text into a cartoon or comic is another example of adaptation. This transposition method can also be applied in the legal field. We can examine some examples to clarify the potential of some forms of adaptation of legal texts to visual language in communicating with foreigners.

An interesting example, in this sense, is the project "Know Your Rights" created by the MADRE association and the CUNY School of Law. The "Know Your Rights" project is mainly aimed at Syrian refugees moving to Lebanon, Turkey, and Jordan.[8]

When discussing the status of refugees, the problems that come to mind are related to war and the need to have basic needs met, such as security or food. However, many refugee women and children do not have identity documents, and the lack of identification makes it difficult for them to access essential services through official channels. Refugees often do not register marriages and births in the

---

[4] Eco (2000), see also Dusi (2000), p. 28.

[5] Hutcheon (2006), p. 16.

[6] Eco (2003b), p. 400.

[7] Ibid., p. 400. My translation.

[8] Know-Your-Rights Visual Guide for Syrian Refugees. In: MADRE. https://www.madre.org/press-publications/your-support-action/know-your-rights-visual-guide-syrian-refugees. Accessed 6 December 2021.

host countries, as they underestimate their importance in accessing particular benefits and ensuring certain rights.

To address this problem, the MADRE association and the CUNY Law School collaborated on the design and publication of a visual guide to inform refugees about the importance of birth and marriage registration, and to provide information about locally available resources.

Anti-fraud comics, edited by the Immigrant Legal Resource Center (ILRC) in the United States, are another example of a visual guide that transposes legal information into a comic-book format.[9] The ILRC provides information and legal support to migrants, and transposes legal information regarding migrants into a comic booklet. The comics provide information about the most common scams perpetrated against migrants, largely based on false beliefs about US migration law. The comics' protagonists are irregular migrants who experience various aspects of fraud and eventually come to understand the deception due to the support of professional lawyers who clarify the actual legal framework. These brochures provide information regarding how immigrants can avoid some of the most common scams, which are often based on false beliefs about US migration law. On one hand, the scammers contribute to the dissemination of false information; on the other hand, they exploit certain aspects of US law, such as triggering a procedure for the deportation of migrants that prevents the victims from reacting effectively against the scammer. The Spanish language version (and its English translation) describe "The 10 Year Benefit/Cancellation of Removal Scam" and "the New Amnesty Scam," while the Chinese version (and its English translation) describe the "job certification scam" and the "disability renunciation scam for naturalization."[10]

The creation of comic contracts is a practice pertaining to the use of adaptations in the legal field. These contractual forms are one of the most innovative products of legal design.

Comic contracts transpose the verbal contractual agreement into a comic. Among the examples most frequently cited in the literature on comic contracts are employment contracts that translate the different elements of the contractual relationship as drawings; for example, duties, working hours, remuneration, and methods for performing the work duties. These elements are described in words in traditional contracts.

These comics are not simply documents that have been prepared to inform the contracting parties about contractual terms, but are sources of obligations and valid legal documents. The contractors can sign the comic contract, following which the comic contract will have the same binding force as a traditional contract. As Haapio and Passera stated with regard to comic contracts:

---

[9] Anti-Fraud Comics | Immigrant Legal Resource Centre | ILRC 2011. https://www.ilrc.org/anti-fraud-comics. Accessed 5 January 2022.

[10] Anti-Fraud Comics | Immigrant Legal Resource Center | ILRC 2011. https://www.ilrc.org/anti-fraud-comics. Accessed 5 January 2022.

> The meaning arises from text and visuals coming together to create a narrative. They cannot be separated: The comic is the contract. [11]

Robert de Rooy and his team combined text and comic artwork to simplify the content of agreements and to make contractual terms accessible to audiences with limited literacy or linguistic skills. [12] A comic contract can be considered to be the multimodal product of the adaptation of a monomodal verbal text. Drafting a contract begins with a verbal interaction between the contracting parties. The contractual terms that were originally expressed verbally are then translated into comics. The source and the target representamen do not have the same binding force, nor the same legal relevance. The source representamen, the verbal interaction, is not binding because it could only be a source of pre-contractual liability. Once signed by the contracting parties, the target representamen (the comic contract) will be legally binding and will have legal effects. [13]

The reverse process of adaptation, translating a legally binding text into a graphic representation of legal norms with a descriptive function, is surely more frequent. Legal innovations are also often communicated via animations or videos. For instance, a video providing an introduction on the Digital Services Act and the Digital Markets Act., available on the official YouTube channel of the EU,[14] can be considered an intersemiotic legal translation.

In the legal field, an adaptation is usually a heterofunctional intersemiotic translation.

An example that we considered previously (Sect. 4.2) is the brochure *Vendor Power*. The artist and urban planner, Candy Chang, translated the most commonly violated rules that regulate street vendors' activities in New York in graphic form via comics and diagrams.[15] In addition to the English version, the brochure has been translated into the most common languages spoken by foreign workers, namely Arabic, Bengali, Chinese, and Spanish. Furthermore, the guide briefly tells the story of street trading in New York and the personal stories of the vendors. Finally, the authors of the brochure formulate considerations and proposals for a reform of the regulation of street trade.

An interesting example of an adaptation that can be included in the heterofunctional intersemiotic legal translation category is represented by the popular videos made by UNHCR to clarify the peculiarities of the status of foreigners in terms of international law.

The use of images in legal communication is a powerful tool for disseminating information about the specifics of the status of foreigners in terms of international

[11] Haapio and Passera (2021), p. 225.

[12] Murray (2021).

[13] Loddo (2020).

[14] The video can be accessed and viewed by navigating to the URL, https://youtu.be/7BW1rXEIEDA.

[15] Barton et al. (2022).

law. [16] As part of the "Teaching about Refugees" project, UNHCR has produced a series of animated short movies aimed at clarifying the peculiarities and differences relating to the statuses of refugees, asylum seekers, migrants, and stateless persons. The short videos can be viewed on the UNHCR's YouTube channel, and reveal the essential elements of international legislation and the fundamental differences among the four different statuses.[17]

A further interesting, heterofunctional form of adaptation was created by the Belgian legal communication agency Droits Quotidiens,[18] which redesigned a document intended for people under arrest and aimed at clarifying their rights and duties. The agency created the brochure through collaboration with the police; the project led to the creation of a prototype in 2022.[19]

5.2.2 Intersemiotic Translation as Illustration

The translation scholar Nilce M. Pereira proposed the idea of intersemiotic translation as illustration:

> Illustrations can especially be seen as translations because, as a process, the methodologies employed by illustrators are, in the majority of cases, the same as those adopted by translators to translate a text. [20]

Translators and illustrators share common procedures[21] in their respective activities, such as addition, omission, emphasizing unexpressed contents, condensation, amplification, and diffusion.[22] According to Pereira, illustration implies the decision to represent part of the source text graphically to facilitate the reader's understanding.

In contrast to adaptation, intersemiotic translation involves a stronger connection between the source and target representamens.

According to Eco, some forms of illustration could be understood as parasynonyms. Eco used the term parasynonymy to indicate "specific cases of interpretation in which, to clarify the meaning of a word or a sentence, is used an

[16] Refugees UNHC for Teaching about Refugees. In: UNHCR. https://www.unhcr.org/teaching-about-refugees.html. Accessed 5 January 2022.

[17] Ibid.

[18] Droits Quotidiens - Le langage juridique clair. https://www.droitsquotidiens.be/fr. Accessed 24 October 2022.

[19] Beaujean O (2022) Le legal design appliqué à la Déclaration de droits lors de l'arrestation. *Legal Design Roundtable*. 29.04.2022. See also Colos F (2021) Improving access to criminal justice, by rewriting the Belgian letter of rights – Clarity. In: Clarity. https://www.clarity-international.org/articles/improving-access-to-criminal-justice-by-rewriting-the-belgian-letter-of-rights/. Accessed 24 October 2022.

[20] Pereira (2008), p. 105.

[21] Pereira (2021), p. 622.

[22] Malone (1988).

interpretant expressed in a different semiotic matter (or vice versa)." [23] An example of parasynonymy is a sentence expressing the meaning of a non-verbal signal, such as a "no smoking" sign.

In fact, the purpose of intersemiotic translation in this case is not only to clarify the meaning of the source text, but also to highlight certain parts of it.

The use of illustrations in the legal field is not new. An interesting example of illustration in the legal field is Eike von Repgow's *Sachsenspiegel*, which is essentially a book of medieval law in which the verbal codification of customary rules is accompanied by exquisite miniatures illustrating the text's most important points.[24]

Unlike adaptation, an illustration, as an intersemiotic translation, does not create a separate and independent work of art, but incorporates the original text instead.

In the field of inheritance law, a famous testament created by the Italian painter Luca Riva provides a good example of an illustration.

In reality, Luca Riva's will, which dates back to 1624, is the product of a double intersemiotic legal translation. In fact, the painter was deaf, could not speak, and had communicated his wishes to the notary via the aid of gestures. The notary wrote the verbal part of the testament, and the painter illustrated the document with drawings. The images, with captions quoting the verbalized will, represent different institutions (churches or convents) or people (relatives or friends) to whom Riva intended to allocate the assets of the inheritance.[25]

Clearly, illustration, particularly in the legal field, is not necessarily composed of pictures. A variety of different tools can be used to illustrate legal content, such as flow charts, organization charts, and Venn diagrams.[26]

An illustration can also be a cartoon, particularly in the digital world. For example, a short, animated video can illustrate the contractual conditions that are spelled out in the written digital legal document. In this regard, the user agreement proposed by the LinkedIn social platform is partially illustrated by a video, which appears both on the company's YouTube channel and on the company's website above the online agreement. The video clarifies some conditions of the user agreement that govern the relationship between the company and the platform's users; in particular, the video refers to the services offered by the platform, intellectual property management, and content management. Unlike a comic contract, this translation is heterofunctional because it does not have the same function as the source text: The video refers explicitly to the user agreement and does not aim to replace it.[27] Illustrations can also have a conceptual function in the legal field. [28] For example, a diagram or a drawing can illustrate how to fulfill an obligation or can

[23] Eco (2003b), p. 372. Also see Eco (2000), pp. 79; 91.

[24] Letts (1933).

[25] De Muro and Imperiale (2021), pp. 32–33.

[26] Murray (2020); Annola et al. (2021).

[27] LinkedIn (2014) LinkedIn User Agreement | Who owns your content? You do. https://www.youtube.com/watch?v=ha7ASaPnjbA. Accessed 15 November 2021.

[28] Moroni and Lorini (2021), pp. 4–5.

clarify a meaning that is not ontic but deontic. In particular, diagrams can perform this task by providing a visual overview of complex concepts or processes. They can break down the different steps involved in fulfilling an obligation, and can also show the different relationships among the various elements of an agreement and how they combine. Moreover, they can simplify the interpreter's work by highlighting the main aspects of a regulation and emphasizing its key elements. They can also highlight the requirements, actions, or events involved in fulfilling an obligation.

Furthermore, diagrams and drawings can increase cognitive processes by engaging visual and spatial thinking. They can facilitate understanding by presenting information in a format that is easier to process and remember. By visualizing the connections among different elements, such as individuals, organizations, and societal norms, diagrams can show how obligations arise, interact, and are fulfilled within a given context. This contextualization helps to clarify the deontic meaning by illustrating the broader socio-legal framework and the interplay of obligations within it. Finally, other forms of visual representation have the potential to extend beyond language and cultural barriers because they can convey information that enables individuals from different linguistic or cultural backgrounds to understand and interpret obligations and the fulfillment thereof. In this regard, diagrams can facilitate cross-cultural dialogue and comprehension, and can contribute to a clearer understanding of deontic meaning.

The intersemiotic illustration of procedural rules can be presented clearly via a cartoon or a diagram.[29]

Moreover, a contract clause that imposes terms, deadlines, and due dates can be represented by a timeline.[30]

In fact, Helena Haapio[31] pointed out that illustration was particularly important in legal contexts by presenting an example of how a graphic representation could have prevented an 18-month administrative dispute, resolved by the CRTC, Canadian Radio-television and Telecommunications Commission, between two major companies (Rogers Communications Inc. vs. Aliant Inc.)[32] In fact, the conflict between the two companies was rooted in the misunderstanding of an ambiguous clause:

[29] Moroni and Lorini (2021), p. 327; Lorini (2019), p. 73.

[30] Various tools for visualizing the contractual clauses which are able to translate some types of contractual clauses in graphic form are being developed. An example of a contract clause visualization tool is accessible online at the following link: Michael Curtotti Research School of Computer Science. https://users.cecs.anu.edu.au/~Michael.Curtotti/tools.htm. Accessed 29 October 2022. An example of a contract clause visualization tool. See Passera et al. (2014).

[31] Haapio (2013).

[32] "For details of the case see Telecommunications Decisions CRTC 2006-45 and CRTC 2007-75, archived at http://www.crtc.gc.ca/eng/archive/2006/dt2006-45.htm and http://www.crtc.gc.ca/eng/archive/2007/dt2007-75.htm. I would like to thank Helena Haapio and Leila Hamhoum for providing me with this reference.

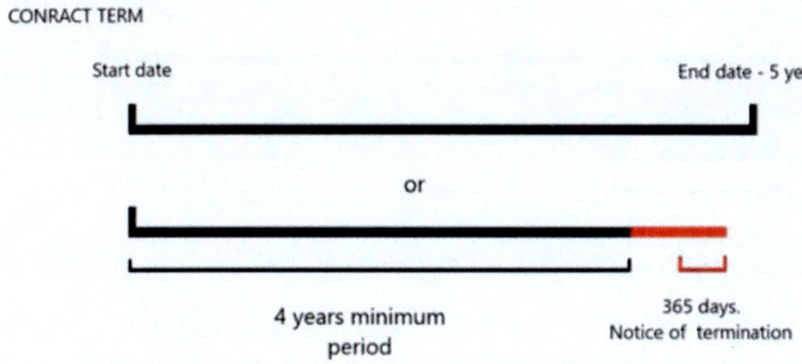

Fig. 5.1 Rogers' understanding. The contract is valid for an initial period of five years. Either party can terminate the contract by giving a year's notice one year prior to the end of this period. From Stefania Passera and Helena Haapio (2011) figure 1. Used with permission. Author rendering. Courtesy of Michael Curtotti, Helena Haapio and Stefania Passera [For details and references, see Haapio and Siedel (2013). A first graphic interpretation of the contractual clause by Stefania Passera originally appeared in Stefania Passera and Helena Haapio (2011)]

> The agreement shall continue in force for a period of five years from the date it is made, and thereafter for successive five-year terms, unless and until terminated by one year prior notice in writing by either party.[33]

Rogers thought that the contract was valid for an initial period of five years. One year prior to the end of this period, either party could terminate the contract by giving one year's notice.

Aliant believed that the agreement could be terminated at any time with one year's notice. I will not go into detail about this litigation. [34] Of course, the clause could have been formulated more clearly; for example, it could have been divided into two sentences. However, the clause could be clarified via a timeline (Figs. 5.1 and 5.2).

A graphic illustration would have been clearer and would have captured the parties' attention better than any verbal expression could have done. [35]

Illustrations can be used in different legal documents. A graph can clarify terms and procedures, and a photograph can show the goods to be sold. Hierarchical relationships within a workplace can be clarified through diagrams. In particular, tree diagrams can be used to illustrate a company's hierarchical structure; for example, they can help to clarify the role played by a worker in the company. A chart can illustrate the technical characteristics of an asset being traded. Flowcharts are useful for illustrating clauses describing processes in which different decisions lead to possible alternative outcomes. Furthermore, they can be used to clarify

[33] Adams (2006) Costly Drafting Errors, Part 1—Rogers Communications and Aliant. In: Adams on Contract Drafting. https://www.adamsdrafting.com/costly-drafting-errors-part-1/. Accessed 24 October 2022.

[34] Haapio and Siedel (2013), pp. 166–167; Passera and Haapio (2011).

[35] Haapio (2013).

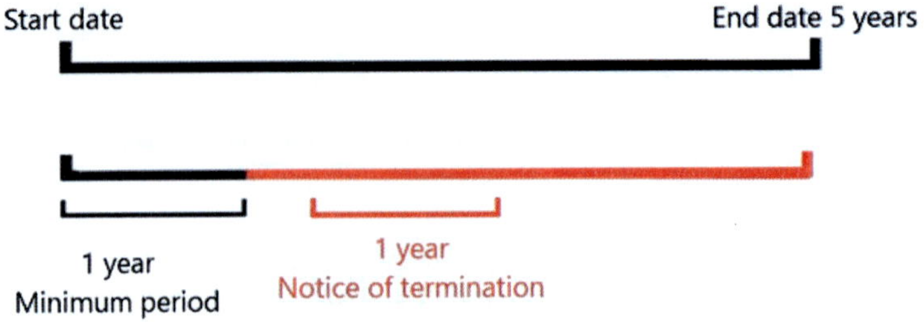

Fig. 5.2 Aliant's understanding. The five-year contract can be terminated at any time with one year's notice. From Stefania Passera and Helena Haapio (2011) figure 1. Used with permission. Author rendering. Courtesy of Michael Curtotti, Helena Haapio and Stefania Passera

complicated evaluation processes in public competitions by highlighting a series of intermediate steps.[36]

Building plans are an integral part of the building sale contract,[37] and are considered to be a binding declaration by the Italian Court of Cassation. In this case, the plan of the building is an illustration that translates the object of the written contract intersemiotically.

5.2.3 Intersemiotic Translation as Resemiotization

The idea of resemiotization focuses on both the function and the material dimension of the translation. According to Iedema, "resemiotization is about how meaning-making shifts from context to context, from practice to practice, or from one stage of a practice to the next."[38] In this regard, Iedema stated:

> Resemiotization is crucially interested in how materiality ('expression') serves to realize the social, cultural, and historical structures, investments, and circumstances of our time.[39]

Scholars who support this concept of intersemiotic translation focus their investigations on the strategic use of intersemiotic translation. An example of intersemiotic translation as resemiotization was provided by Bruno Latour, who described the semiotic history of some artifacts, such as automatic door closers. [40]

Latour uses the terms "shifting" and "delegation" to describe the shifting of meaning from a situation in which someone asks those who enter a room to close

---

[36] See Sect. 4.2.

[37] Italian Court of Cassation. Sent. n.26366/2016.

[38] Iedema (2003), p. 41.

[39] Ibid., p. 51.

[40] Latour (1992), p. 229.

the door behind them to a written notice reading "Please keep this door closed" to the development of an automatic door closing device. [41]

As Iedema pointed out, Latour's attention in this case was focused on intersemiotic shifts ranging from the linguistic act to the creation of a technological device.[42] More specifically, in this example, we are observing a transition from a speech act (or a document act)[43] that expresses rules or directives (*a normative linguistic act*) to a technological device that pertains to material possibilities or impossibilities. Thus we are shifting from a deontic dimension to an ontic one.

The examples proposed by Latour have attracted the interest of scholars whose research focuses on normativity. Lorini and Moroni stated that, despite losing their original normative sense from a semiotic point of view, some artifacts still maintain a regulatory function. In this regard, the two authors discussed "regulation without rules" or "rule-free regulation" to indicate all those cases in which "desired or undesired behaviors are not" codified "in prescriptive rules, but are favored (or disfavored) options within an appropriately framed anomic and adeontic environment."[44] Lorini and Moroni mentioned several examples of rule-free regulations, such as the anti-homeless devices typical of so-called hostile architecture.

In this sense, benches with metal dividers or with an uneven surface, which are unusable for any purpose other than sitting, and metal studs implanted in the ground to discourage people from lingering in certain places, make unwanted intersemiotic legal translation behavior impossible. The regulatory aim of these artifacts is identical to that of a verbal norm that prohibits lying down in certain places; however, they do not have a normative dimension because they cannot be violated. Moreover, a physical device (or even the provision of the installation of physical devices) can hardly be considered formally as being in contradiction to higher legal (or moral) norms.

There is a clear distinction between Latour's approach and the approach presented by Lorini and Moroni. While Latour discusses technological tools that may not necessarily have regulatory functions, Lorini and Moroni specifically emphasize instruments that are designed to regulate human behavior in either a deontic or an adeontic manner.

The concept of resemiotization can also be a key to interpreting the application of verbal legal norms. In fact, from a material fact (for example, Mark shoots John dead), the interpreter reverts to the verbal juridical norm (such as Article 575 of the Italian Criminal Code that punishes murder) to arrive at the material dimension with the execution of the legal decision.

However, taking the example proposed by Latour[45] into consideration, in light of the idea of "rule-free regulations" proposed by Lorini and Moroni, we acknowledge

---

[41] Latour (1992); Iedema (2003).

[42] Iedema (2003), p. 43.

[43] Smith (2014).

[44] Lorini and Moroni (2021), p. 3.

[45] Latour (1992).

that the phenomenon of resemiotization can lead to a significant loss of meaning in the final artifact. [46] In other words, by following the example proposed by Latour and adopted by Iedema, the process of resemiotization can lead to the creation of an artifact (target) through an intersemiotic translation process which, while preserving the regulatory nature of the source text, loses the original normative meaning.

5.3 Intersemiotic Legal Translation as Transactional Process

With regard to the concept of intersemiotic translation as a transactional process, the emphasis is on the cultural dimension of the translation; this dimension has been investigated extensively in the context of interlingual translation. [47]

According to Torop:

> Translating as an activity and translation as the result of this activity are inseparable from the concept of culture. The translational capacity of culture is an important criterion of culture's specificity. Culture operates largely through translational activity, since only by the inclusion of new texts into culture can the culture undergo innovation as well as perceive its specificity.[48]

Translation determines the triggering of a cultural exchange mechanism; more precisely, the translator becomes a cultural mediator who initiates an exchange process between the source's author and the translation's recipients.[49]

Intersemiotic translation is essential in intercultural communication. Semiotic choices are translated into social practices over time and thus acquire a pragmatic and multimodal dimension.

According to the Sapir-Whorf hypothesis, each language expresses a different vision of the world; this implies important limits to the possibility of translating from one language to another. This might lead us to consider translating from a different semiotic system even more difficult, yet we resort to non-linguistic semiotic resources when words are lacking because the linguistic communities underlying non-verbal languages are often wider than the linguistic communities; thus, intersemiotic translators can search for a non-verbal language that is shared by multiple nations and adapt it to their purpose. Consider the diversity of forms of

---

[46] Lorini and Moroni (2020); Lorini and Moroni (2021).

[47] See, for example, Borutti and Heidmann (2012).

[48] Torop (2002), p. 593.

[49] Despite mainly referring to interlingual legal translation, Ricca (2023) emphasized the importance of intercultural translation in legal practice, and suggested that lawyers should promote intercultural understanding.

visual communication, such as international road signs, pictorial guides, colors,[50] visual storytelling, infographics (which display complex data and statistics in a visually appealing way), and signed languages that incorporate gestures and facial expressions.[51] This aspect of translation, which has already been discussed in interlingual translations, is particularly prominent in intersemiotic translations; for example, the intersemiotic translation of written rules as images usually aims to simplify the interpretation of the rules for users from different cultural backgrounds: An intersemiotic translation from written text into multimodal text that includes visual elements, such as colors, shapes, and symbols, can carry widely recognized meanings and associations across different cultures.[52] Moreover, visual information can be processed more quickly and intuitively than written or verbal language. Images, diagrams, and symbols can convey complex concepts or instructions in a concise and easily understandable manner.[53]

According to Campbell and Vidal, intersemiotic translation inevitably creates connections between different cultures. Intersemiotic translation is a transactional process, as both the author of the source text and the recipient of the translation can understand the code used to translate the source text perfectly.[54]

This concept of intersemiotic translation highlights a fundamental aspect of intersemiotic legal translation: the intersemiotic translation of a verbal legal norm can help to overcome the lack of a shared natural language in a legal community.[55]

This is relevant for legal design, where attention is paid to the potential addressees of the legal message and to their cultural background. This leads to the choice of a communication channel that gives the recipient a full (or better) understanding of the message. A sign identified by international conventions, such as a prohibition sign, or which has been spontaneously shared through international cultural channels (comics, cinema, animated drawings, or music) will be more easily understood by a foreigner than will a verbal expression that is known only within a specific linguistic community or that can be traced back to a technical language known only to a few experts.

Intersemiotic translation operates beyond rigid guidelines, and employs established conventions as strategic tools instead. While the governing of the grammatical structures of non-linguistic communication practices extend beyond national borders, they can still pose cultural obstacles. In such situations, intersemiotic translation emerges as an invaluable resource for surmounting these barriers, thus allowing for enhanced understanding and cross-cultural exchange.

---

[50] Colors can be used to convey information or evoke specific meanings. For example, in a safety manual, important warnings or hazards may be highlighted using the color red, which is widely associated with danger or caution.

[51] Sapir (1949); Whorf (1964).

[52] Van Leeuwen (2005).

[53] Nutting (1964).

[54] Campbell and Vidal (2019).

[55] Haapio (2013).

5.4 Conclusion

Words are not the only possible channel for legal communication. This fact is obvious in everyday life: We constantly encounter forms of non-verbal communication that are intended to facilitate and accelerate the understanding of a regulatory message in airports, stations, streets, public places, or in digital environments. Other examples of this are tactile signals intended for the deaf or acoustic signals intended for the blind, road signs, and icons that are present in the various forms of signage in public places or on institutional web platforms. Both those who navigate the web and those who travel by sea or by land must be able to understand what they can or cannot do quickly and easily.

Non-verbal channels can become vectors of normative communication. Clearly, the intricate essence and innate potential bestowed by legal language elude complete encapsulation within non-verbal realms of expression. However, images, drawings, diagrams, and cartoons can be a useful tool for facilitating the understanding of a legal message, thus making it also accessible to people who have different legal and linguistic contexts. For example, the system of road signs has been introduced specifically for the purpose of ensuring that travelers travel in a safe and secure manner, in compliance with the regulations in force, on the roads of foreign countries in which they do not speak the language. Foreigners are among the main users of these forms of legal communication since, in addition to not knowing the legal institutions that regulate the life of the country in which they are located, they often do not share the same mother tongue as the legislator. In particular, the issue of legal communication with foreigners has attracted the interest of legal design scholars.

Legal communication through the use of semiotic channels in addition to words is enriched with new tools that are aimed at breaking down the linguistic barriers that are often the precondition of legal and cultural barriers.

In this regard, foreigners can take advantage of the adoption of these legal communication strategies that are centered on the recipient.

Non-linguistic communication channels can be used to provide information about foreigners' rights and obligations (immigrants, asylum seekers, refugees, stateless people, and so forth), and can facilitate their integration into a (temporary or permanent) legal and cultural context. Non-linguistic communication channels may, for example, illustrate how foreigners can benefit from certain institutions, help them to defend themselves against scams, and facilitate their integration into a specific work environment in the country in which they are residing. Simply knowing that a particular institution exists in the country of residence can be essential for a foreigner.

Using a widespread communication channel can be intended to promote integration by breaking down linguistic barriers; however, the inclusive nature of a channel does not necessarily reflect the content of the rule. The use of intersemiotic translation in the legal field is not necessarily aimed at promoting integration. It seems clear that a discriminatory rule, even if represented through comics, does not change its nature. This is the case of the comic strips published in the magazine *La difesa della razza* (*The Defense of the Race*).[56] These comic strips are an adaptation aimed at clarifying the rules that came into force in Italy during the fascist regime in 1938.

The inclusive character of the graphic representation of norms concerns the communicative dimension.

However, it cannot be denied that this practice may represent a factor of potential legal innovation. In fact, even a simply descriptive graphic representation of norms, precisely due to the ability to clarify the discipline of a particular institution, can highlight the emerging problems and issues, and can eventually encourage their reform.

References

Annola V, Haapio H, Koskela M (2021) Interpreting images in contracts. In: Corrales Compagnucci M, Haapio H, Fenwick M (eds) Research handbook on contract design. Elgar, Northampton

Barton TD, Haapio H, Passera S, Hazard JG (2022) Reframing contract design: integrating business, legal, design, and technology perspectives. In: Corrales Compagnucci M, Haapio H, Fenwick (eds) Research handbook on contract design. Edward Elgar Publishing, Northampton

Beaujean O (2022) Le legal design appliqué à la Déclaration de droits lors de l'arrestation. Legal Design Roundtable. 29.04.2022

Borutti S, Heidmann U (2012) La Babele in cui viviamo: Traduzioni, riscritture, culture. Bollati Boringhieri, Torino

Campbell M, Vidal R (2019) The translator's gaze: Intersemiotic translation as transactional process. In: Campbell M, Vidal R (eds) Translating across sensory and linguistic borders. Springer, Cham, pp 1–36

Colos F (2021) Improving access to criminal justice, by rewriting the Belgian letter of rights. In: Clarity. https://www.clarity-international.org/articles/improving-access-to-criminal-justice-by-rewriting-the-belgian-letter-of-rights/. Accessed 24 October 2022.

De Muro B, Imperiale M (2021) Legal design. Come il design può semplificare il diritto. Giuffrè, Milano

Dusi N (2000) Introduzione. Per una ridefinizione della traduzione intersemiotica. Quaderni di studi semiotici 85/86/87:3–54

Dusi N (2015) Intersemiotic translation: theories, problems, analysis. Semiotica 206:181–205. https://doi.org/10.1515/sem-2015-0018

Eco U (2000) Traduzione e interpretazione. Quaderni di studi semiotici 85/86/87:55–100

Eco U (2003a) Mouse or Rat? Translation as negotiation. Phoenix, London

Eco U (2003b) Dire quasi la stessa cosa: Esperienze di traduzione. Bompiani, Milano

Haapio H (2013) Contract clarity and usability through visualization. In: Marchese FT, Banassi E (eds) Knowledge visualization currents. From text to art to culture. Springer, London, pp 63–84

Haapio H, Passera S (2021) Contracts as interfaces: exploring visual representation patterns in contract design. In: Katz DM, Dolin R, Bommarito M (eds) Legal informatics. Cambridge University Press, Cambridge, pp 213–238

Haapio H, Siedel GJ (2013) A short guide to contract risk. Routledge

Hutcheon L (2006) A theory of adaptation. Routledge, New York

[56]The racist comic strip was published in the newspaper "La difesa della razza [The Defense of the Race]" on November the 10th, 1938.

Iedema R (2003) Multimodality, resemiotization: extending the analysis of discourse as multi-semiotic practice. Visual communication 2:29–57. https://doi.org/10.1177/1470357203002001751
Jakobson R (1959) On linguistic aspects of translation. In: Brower RA (ed) On translation. MIT Press, London, pp 232–239
Latour B (1992) Where are the missing masses? The sociology of a few mundane artifacts. In: Bijker WE, Law J (eds) Shaping technology/building society: studies in sociotechnical change. MIT Press, Cambridge, pp 225–258
Letts M (1933) The Sachsenspiegel and its illustrators. Law Quarterly Review 49:555–574
Loddo OG (2020) The background of normative pictures. Archiv für Rechts- und Sozialphilosophie (ARSP) 106:563. https://doi.org/10.25162/arsp-2020-0023
Lorini G (2019) Corporeal drawn norms. An investigation of graphic normativity in the material world of everyday objects. Phenomenology and Mind 17:80–90. https://doi.org/10.13128/pam-8027
Lorini G, Moroni S (2020) Ruling without rules. Regulation beyond normativity. Global Jurist 20: 1–11. https://doi.org/10.1515/gj-2019-0051
Lorini G, Moroni S (2021) Rule-free regulation exploring regulation without rules and apart from deontic. Journal for the Theory of Social Behaviour:1–15. https://onlinelibrary.wiley.com/doi/10.1111/jtsb.12291
Lorini G, Moroni S, Loddo OG (2021) Deontic artifacts. Investigating the normativity of objects. Philosophical Explorations 24:185–203. https://doi.org/10.1080/13869795.2021.1908584
Malone JL (1988) The science of linguistics in the art of translation: some tools from linguistics for the analysis and practice of translation. State University of New York Press, New York
Murray MD (2020) Diagrammatics and the proactive visualization of legal information. University of Arkansas at Little Rock Law Review 43:46
Murray MD (2021) Cartoon contracts and the proactive visualization of law. University of Massachusetts Law Review 16:98–197
Nutting CB (1964) Graphic law. American Bar Association Journal 50:780–781
Passera S, Haapio H (2011) Facilitating collaboration through contract visualization and modularization. In: European conference on cognitive ergonomics ECCE. Rostock, Germany, pp 57–60
Passera S, Curtotti M, Haapio H (2014) Making the meaning of contracts visible – automating contract visualization. In: Schweighofer E (ed) Transparenz IRIS 2014: Tagungsband des 17. Internationalen Rechtsinformatik Symposions. Österreichische Computer-Ges, Wien, pp 443–450
Pereira NM (2008) Book illustration as (Intersemiotic) translation: pictures translating words. Meta 53:104–119. https://doi.org/10.7202/017977ar
Pereira NM (2021) Translational functions of book illustrations, and what Dickens has to do with them. In: Ferstl P (ed) Dialogues between Media. De Gruyter, Boston, pp 621–638 https://doi.org/10.1515/9783110642056-046
Queiroz J, Aguiar D (2015) C. S. Peirce and Intersemiotic Translation. In: International Handbook of Semiotics. P. P. Trifonas, pp 201–215
Ricca M (2023) Intercultural spaces of Law: translating invisibilities. Springer, Cham
Sapir E (1949) Selected writings of Edward Sapir in language, culture, and personality. University of California Press, Berkeley
Smith B (2014) Document acts. In: Konzelmann-Ziv A, Schmid HB (eds) Institutions, emotions, and group agents: contributions to social ontology. Springer, Dordrecht, pp 19–31 https://doi.org/10.1007/978-94-007-6934-2_2
Torop P (2002) Translation as translating as culture. Sign Systems Studies 30:593–605. https://doi.org/10.12697/SSS.2002.30.2.14
Van Leeuwen T (2005) Introducing social semiotics. Routledge, London
Whorf BL (1964) Language, thought, and reality: selected writings. The MIT Press, Cambridge

Chapter 6
Intersemiotic Digital Legal Translation

6.1 Introduction

In recent years, digital devices have become fundamental tools for intersemiotic translation. At present, most intersemiotic translations are carried out using technological tools and transmitted via the internet. Technical complexity has long prevented intersemiotic translation from becoming relevant in the same manner as interlingual translation. For example, everyone can learn how to write or read, but few know how to draw.[1] However, technological advancements are gradually making it possible to overcome this obstacle. As early as the 1980s, Plaza, in his analysis of intersemiotic translation, stated prophetically:

> The technological tools absorb and incorporate the most widely differing sign systems by translating the different historical languages into new supports.[2]

The phenomenon that Plaza described has developed exponentially over the last forty years. The use of social media involves both multimodal communication and intersemiotic translation, and we compose multimodal texts every day: We may sometimes use emojis or GIFs to translate information that was previously expressed via words.

In general, technological developments over the past few decades have improved people's abilities to communicate and to express themselves.

Digital communication technologies have allowed us to interact with others through machines by amplifying our abilities to draw on different semiotic resources that are capable of interacting with multiple sensory dimensions. According to Plaza,

> [i]mages and texts appear as icons of speech translated into images of the scansion movement of writing. We see the speech; we hear the image. The tactility of writing forms an image with the translation (via modem) of bits into images. These transcoded languages

[1] Boehme-Neßler (2011).

[2] Plaza (1987), p. 65. My translation.

O. G. Loddo, *Intersemiotic Legal Translation*, Law and Visual Jurisprudence 11,
https://doi.org/10.1007/978-3-031-44184-4_6

> produce a collaboration between the different senses, enabling the creative intersemiotic transit between visual, verbal, acoustic, and tactile.[3]

The process of transposing natural language into machine language in digital environments produces intersemiotic translations. As Plaza stated:

> Web interfaces are a product of qualitative synthesis, a combination of the computer, domestic video, and the cabling that allows the display of texts and images using telematics (computers plus communication networks). Thus, text-images circulate on the web through the computer's memories and are displayed in the video, as requested by the user. There is a plurality of support, and the image shown is mere potential that appears when requested.[4]

The internet allows us to perform *digital speech acts* that can be legally relevant (*digital legal acts*). We communicate and accept contract proposals with the click of a mouse. We can easily create an e-commerce site using a content management system that will allow us to manage digital payments. We can make payments (wire transfers, postal slips, or other forms of money transfers) through the internet banking service made available by our bank. We can archive documents by digitalizing them and uploading them to blockchains to ensure their integrity. We can even translate a contractual clause into a smart contract to allow automatic execution when certain conditions are met. Until recently, all these acts could only be accomplished through words: We can now digitalize these activities and make them faster, easier, more accessible, and more efficient. The performance of a legal act in a digital environment develops in a complex chain of events that includes the identification of a set of possible legal acts made available to the user by the platform manager, the creation of an interface based on the platform manager's choices, the user's choice based on the options proposed in the interface, and the input sent to the machine and its translation into a machine code/structured format.[5]

6.2 The Web Developer as a "Legal" Intersemiotic Translator

Intersemiotic translations are a fundamental element in the development of web interfaces. The web developer (or the development team) manages the translation flow from the machine to the user by creating digital interfaces with which the user will need to interact.

> The developer (or a development team) [. . .] starting from more or less abstract programming, markup, or scripting language, or through more refined tools, creates an interface to allow the user to interact with the owner of the service offered. The developer necessarily cooperates with the web designer, who, especially through markup and scripting languages,

[3] Ibid., pp. 65–66. My translation.

[4] Ibid., p. 66. My translation.

[5] Addis and Loddo (2022).

> through a [content management system] CMS, creates a graphic interface aimed at allowing the user to interact with the company that owns the website.[6]

In the early days of the World Wide Web, the user was simply a recipient of the intersemiotic translation performed by a machine. It was mainly a one-way communication process. At that time, organizing information to convey the message to the user most effectively and efficiently was the key aspect of the developer's tasks.

The advent of Web 2.0 enabled users to play active roles in intersemiotic translations.[7]

This change has affected the development of the user interface design of digital platforms. The user's interface must not only convey information, but must also be designed to enable the user to operate on the platform. In a digital environment, some of the actions the user can perform are legal acts, which is why the interface must be designed to make the platform user-friendly.

6.3 The User as a Legal Intersemiotic Translator

A speaker of a particular language performs a number of speech acts, "such as making statements, giving commands, asking questions, and making promises."[8]

Starting from Wittgenstein's investigation of the different language uses, J. L. Austin[9] and J. R. Searle[10] developed a theory of speech acts and of their relevance in the construction of social reality. Speech acts have been extensively analyzed by contemporary philosophers of language. The importance of speech acts has also been analyzed by legal philosophers, who have identified a strong connection between this typology of acts and legal acts. According to the Swedish lawyer and legal philosopher Karl Olivecrona, legal acts produce constitutive legal effects, which have a psychic nature.[11] More recently, other scholars have noticed that semiotic tools other than words, such as drawings, can produce norms and shape social reality.[12]

What we are interested in emphasizing here is that analogous acts can be performed in a digital environment; these acts can produce legal effects and shape social reality.

In order to be performed, they require an intersemiotic transposition from natural language to machine language.

---

[6]Ibid., p. 276.

[7](Sykora (2017)

[8]Searle (1969), p. 16.

[9]Austin (1953).

[10]Searle (1989).

[11]In fact, Austin's vision was revisited by Olivecrona (1971), who had the merit of combining the theory of performativity with the theory of legal acts.

[12]Lorini and Moroni (2020).

In fact, it is possible to perform speech acts[13] in digital environments[14]. Digital speech acts[15] are performed through intersemiotic translations and produce legal effects. Users can interact with a web platform and carry out their own digital intersemiotic legal translations via the use of technological resources. In this case, the users exploit the instruments offered by the machine not only to translate their legal intentions into a digital dimension, but also to perform acts. For example, the conclusion of an electronic contract makes it indispensable for the contractor to transpose the contractual will into machine language through an intersemiotic translation process.[16]

In electronic contracts,[17] the user-contractor concludes the agreement through an input device, such as a click on a button on the digital interface using the left mouse button. The same act would have traditionally been performed in words, with a signature, or with a simple handshake. The interaction between the user and the platform can produce *legal* and *financial effects*. Thus, at least four types of output can represent the product of intersemiotic translation in the digital environment, namely epistemic effects, legal effects, digital effects, and financial effects.[18]

As Addis and Loddo stated:

> Through intersemiotic translation of a legal document, the legal content can be made more accessible even to non-specialized users (epistemic effect). A digital document can produce legal effects. For instance, this is the case of platforms for the compilation of legally valid contractual documents. The process can be supported by tools such as Contract lifecycle management (CLM) software, i.e., contract tools that help professionals to create, negotiate, sign, renew, and analyze contracts.[19]

It is important to note that intersemiotic translations are at the root of these acts. In the previous chapter (Sect. 3.4), we discussed the fact that intersemiotic translation has an extremely distinct creative dimension, and that part of the semantic content of the source representamen can be lost in translation.

Brownsword described a diachronic transformation of the legal world using technological and digital developments as keys to the understanding of the transformation of the modes of regulation. In the Law 3.0. stage, the new technologies become new regulatory tools[20] that have a causal impact on human behavior. In other words, such tools do not have a normative meaning *per se*, but are designed to affect human behavior physically. Therefore, they do not imply a choice to follow a

[13] Searle (1969).

[14] Addis et al. (2021).

[15] Searle (1969); Smith (2014).

[16] Glatt (1998); Blount (2015).

[17] Marzotto (2008).

[18] Loddo et al. (2022).

[19] Addis and Loddo (2022), p. 277.

[20] Brownsword (2019); Brownsword (2021).

rule on the part of the subject; they do not have propositional content,[21] but have a purely causal effect.

Some effects in the non-digital dimension of the act should have a legal nature, but acquire a digital-material nature due to the intersemiotic translation.

Blockchain platform developers have created simplified (compared to traditional high-level languages) domain-specific programming languages to allow users with basic computer knowledge to create smart contracts.

Smart contracts are a particular form of the intersemiotic translation of contractual clauses into software to realize contractual intentions, which are converted into machine language. In this case, the machine is a tool that allows the user to digitize their contractual relationship.

Nick Szabo, who is considered to have created the smart contract, defined it as "a computerized transaction protocol that executes the terms of a contract."[22]

Based on the definition of the smart contract, it is possible to deduce that the protocols of smart contracts could be considered to be a target text, whereas the source text is the set of contractual terms. As stated by Cervone, Palmirani, and Vitali:

> [A] Smart Contract is considered a specific interpretation and translation (a codification) of its corresponding legal prose, which is the written expression of a mutual assent about the contractual terms (e.g., the considerations of a contract).[23]

The advantages of this technology were summarized by Szabo, who stated:

> Smart contracts reduce mental and computational transaction costs imposed by either principal, third parties, or their tools. [. . .] This gives us new ways to formalize and secure digital relationships which are far more functional than their inanimate paper-based ancestors.[24]

A smart contract is a resource that should be considered carefully by lawyers who are more attentive to the application of new technologies to meet the needs of business and contract management.[25] There are certain hermeneutical limitations of smart contracts; these limitations are related to the fact that the contractual document is separate from the smart code, thus making it impossible to understand the nature of the transaction solely on the basis of code.

It is possible to draft smart contracts using graphic symbols or to translate smart contracts interlinguistically between different programming languages. In this regard, it is worth mentioning the Marlowe Playground, which is a tool for drafting smart contracts provided by the Cardano platform. Marlowe Playground (Fig. 6.1)

---

[21] Lorini and Moroni (2022).

[22] Szabo (1997).

[23] Cervone et al. (2020).

[24] Szabo (1997).

[25] Corrales et al. (2019).

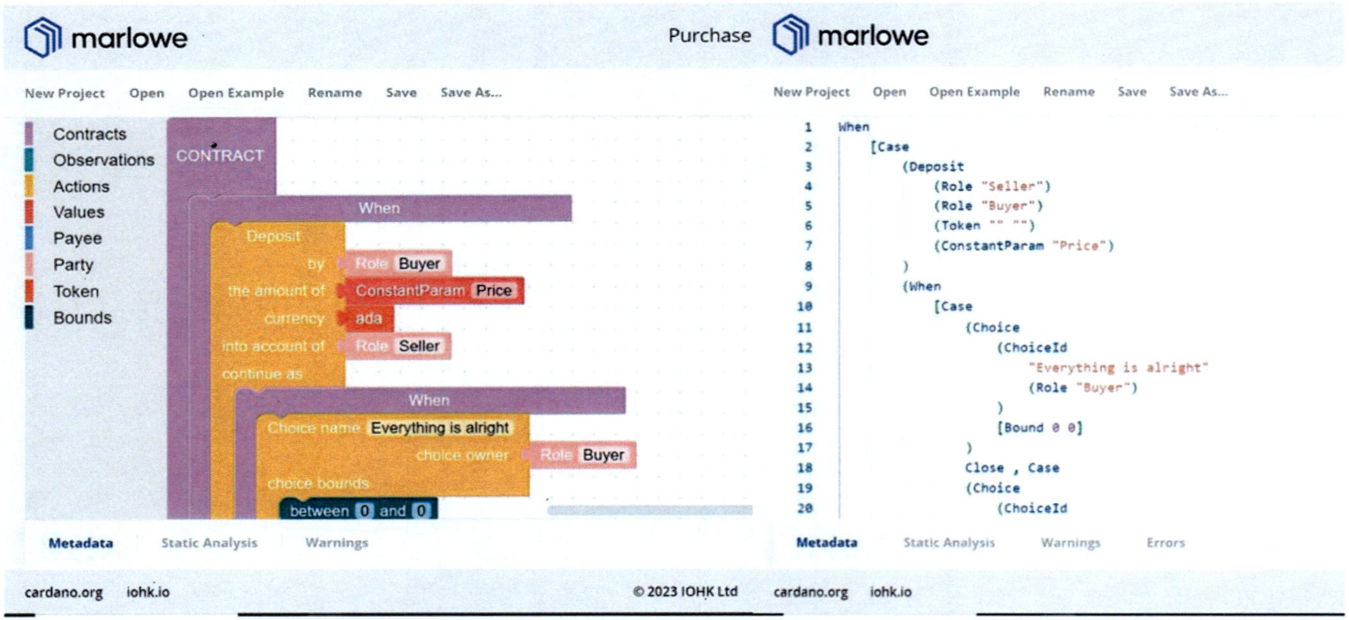

Fig. 6.1 A demonstration from Cardano Playground. The image represents part of an Escrow (translated via Marlow and Blockly) to regulate the money transfer between a buyer and a seller. Marlowe Playground. In: https://play.marlowe.iohk.io/#/. Accessed 4 June 2022. Used with permission. Courtesy of Charles Hoskinson

allows the translation of a smart contract into Haskell, JavaScript, Marlowe, or even into the blocks used in the Blockly language.[26]

However, unlike a traditional contractual text, the smart contract code is not meant to be interpreted by a human being, but only by a machine.

In this regard, the most significant aspect of smart contracts is the intersemiotic translation from natural language to machine language. This translation results in an ontological change in the effects of the contract, which are no longer legal and mediated (since they need no longer to be implemented by another subject), but are financial and immediate; that is, they occur automatically at the time of the program's execution. The software is capable of replacing the parties in fulfilling the contractual obligation. This change is reflected in the effects of the contract, which change from legal (obligations and claims) to economic (a money transfer). More precisely, the drafting of a smart contract could be seen as the translation of a contractual clause from the deontic to the ontic; a clause becomes software that could perform a service regardless of the parties' intervention. This alteration of the nature of the contractual clause has not gone unnoticed, and has raised many doubts among lawyers.[27] For example, Giancaspro pointed out that smart contracts[28] could also give rise to several legal problems.[29] When smart contracts automate the fulfillment of contractual obligations, it may be viewed as a constraint on contractual freedom. Essentially, if both parties execute the agreement in line with their initial intentions and the contract is valid and enforceable, they are exercising their contractual freedom.[30]

> However, if the clauses underlying the smart contract are subject to different interpretations by the contracting parties and it is necessary to ascertain whether the smart contract corresponds to the negotiating program, the freedom from the contract can be lost. In other words, if the planned performance in the smart contract, which is the intersemiotic translation of a contractual clause, differs from that described in the clause and requires the

---

[26]Marlowe Playground. In: https://play.marlowe.iohk.io/#/. Accessed 7 July 2023. The Cardano platform provides the user with the possibility of drafting smart contracts using a simplified programming language (compared to traditional high-level languages) to realize the contractual intentions, which are converted into machine language. In this case, the machine is a tool that allows users to digitize their contractual relationship: See Lamela Seijas and Thompson (2018). In general, smart contracts are created via a simplified programming language that is specific to a particular domain. Correctness and unambiguity are not only essential formal properties, as compliance with any legislation governing the matter involved in the transaction must also be ensured. The reliability, safety, and security of the platform that executes the transactions are the main attributes.

[27]Giancaspro (2017); Governatori et al. (2018).

[28]It is important not to confuse the concept of "smart contract" with that of "smart *legal* contract". Of note, this concept appears in the consultation paper on Digitalon Digital assets | Law Commission. https://www.lawcom.gov.uk/project/digital-assets/. Accessed 16 August 2022 by the Law Commission of England and Wales that defines smart legal contracts as "A legally binding contract in which some or all of the contractual terms are defined in and/or performed automatically by a computer program."

[29]Giancaspro (2017); Also see Cuccuru (2017).

[30]Burton (2009).

> fulfillment of obligations that are not justified by the contract, a series of safeguarding measures that should be guaranteed to contractors are infringed.[31]

In smart contracts, the programming language can translate not only the manifestation (the form) but the entire act (and its effects) in the digital environment. However, when this takes place, the nature of the effects that are produced changes. The effects that originally needed to be mediated (via the fulfillment by the debtor) become immediate consequences which, based on an algorithm, must be produced upon the occurrence of an event. In this sense, the question no longer pertains to legal effects but to digital-financial effects.

6.4 Intersemiotic Digital Translation and Dark Patterns

The user's active role in intersemiotic digital translation has affected the development of the user interface design of online platforms. The user's interface must be designed to enable the user to operate on the platform. In a digital environment, some of the actions the user can perform are legal acts, which is why the interface must be designed to make the platform user-friendly.

It is interesting to note that the choice of one semiotic tool instead of another can have *ethical relevance*. The translators can choose a sign that reconciles their communication needs with the needs and interests of the recipient. However, the platform design may be ineffective if its form is not suitable for the purpose of the translation.

In their book *A unified theory of information design*, Nicole Amare and Alan Manning considered unethical visual forms of communication to be those that

> [p]ursue purposes of its creator that are not jointly shared by the recipients, or purposes that, even if shared jointly, are not achievable or sustainable.[32]

In this assessment, they clearly refer to Peirce's pragmatism. The sign can be *unethical* if it serves the purposes of its creator that are not aligned with those of the recipient of the translation or, if they are shared, are neither feasible nor sustainable.[33]

In fact, according to Amare and Manning, "Peirce proposed a close integration between visual and textual."[34] Regardless of whether the information is based on visual or textual signs, we can only understand the effectiveness of the information in terms of communication objectives; that is, what the author intended to achieve using this sign or another, and what effect a text supported by images has on the public. Peirce defined the rhetorical unfolding of signs, visual or otherwise, in terms of effectiveness, which must be defined in terms of needs, goals, or ends. Consequently, in Peirce's system, a logically necessary connection emerges between ethics and the

---

[31] Loddo et al. (2022), p. 7.

[32] Amare and Manning (2013), p. 2.

[33] Amare and Manning (2013).

[34] Ibid., p. 12.

actual achievement of ends (objectives). In this case, ethics is understood as the study of the ends of the action that we are deliberately willing to deliberately adopt.

For example, using Peirce's analysis, we can explicitly link the bait-and-switch advertising[35] of consumer goods to the ethical problem created by excessively photoshopped images.

The objectives of the visual designer and the recipients of the offer do not align: The visual designer intends to sell goods by representing them in a misleading way to influence the buyer's choices by generating false beliefs based on artificially improved images. These images aim to influence the choices of the potential buyer. Clearly, the visual designers do not share the belief (and consequently the goal) that they themselves have deliberately created in the minds of their audience. In fact, they know that the images that they have artificially created are impossible to achieve in reality.

The development and spread of electronic commerce have made establishing the boundary between a negotiated offer and an advertising text increasingly complex. The interfaces of e-commerce sites often adopt the graphic techniques used in advertising, but these sites are often the main source of information about the characteristics of the goods that the seller offers to the potential buyer. The idea that web interfaces, which are actually the product of an intersemiotic translation, can represent a new form of the contractual document is spreading among civil lawyers.[36]

These interfaces also allow the validity of contracts for which the written form is required provided that the criteria required by law for the identification of the parties are respected.[37] As Corrales Compagnucci, Haapio, and Fenwick stated:

> These changes are enabled by the parties' freedom of contract: the parties are not only free to choose and agree upon the contents of their contract, but they are also free to choose its form (except when the law requires a specific form, such as in the case of the sale of real property).[38]

The use of intersemiotic translation techniques in contract drafting is fully within the scope of freedom of form. However, this exercise of contractual freedom of form can harm one of the parties in some cases by inducing false beliefs through specific web design strategies. In this regard, we can speak of "dark patterns" to indicate interfaces on which web designers consciously confuse users, make it difficult to express actual preferences, push them to perform certain actions that have legally relevant consequences of granting access to their data or assuming certain obligations through manipulation techniques. In general, dark patterns exploit cognitive prejudices or biases and push online consumers to purchase goods and services that they do not want or cause them to reveal personal information that they would prefer not

[35] A "bait and switch" occurs when the seller advertises an offer of good or service that the seller does not actually intend to sell. Instead, the seller offers an alternative that is poor, defective, or different from the one desired by the buyer.

[36] Glatt (1998); Blount (2015); Stazi (2021).

[37] In the US legal system, the electronic contract is assimilated into the written contract and the word evidence rule is considered applicable to it. Burton (2009), p. 72.

[38] Corrales Compagnucci et al. (2022).

to disclose. The manager of an interactive web platform can abuse the freedom of form by exploiting the asymmetry of information, the cognitive biases of users, and their automatic behaviors to induce the other contractor to make certain choices.[39]

The specific characteristics of dark patterns include relying on interfaces to influence and manipulate users, subvert intentions or preferences, and abuse knowledge of human behavior to predict and influence users' decisions. Dark patterns can be based on user profiling or can be implemented on a more general basis by drawing on heuristics and behavioral distortions.[40]

The designer Harry Brignull coined the neologism "dark pattern" in 2010, and created the website darkpatterns.org, a "library of patterns with the specific purpose of reporting deceptive user interfaces."[41] Several examples of dark patterns are mentioned on the Brignull site. One of these is misdirection (wrong direction); in this case, the interface design is structured in such a way as to intentionally focus the users' attention on one thing to distract their attention from another. A good example that Brignull identified was on the website of the low-cost Australian airline Jetstar. The way in which the page presented the options for selecting a seat on the plane was deceptive. When the page dedicated to the choice of seat was loaded, the user would find a pre-selected seat at an additional cost of $ 9 ($ 4.50 each way). This is misleading for two reasons: First, the user has neither chosen nor requested that seat, as the platform has automatically added it to the cart. Second, an extra cost is charged for a seat that has not been chosen and, considering that an extra amount must be paid to be able to choose the seat, the user is paying without receiving consideration. A simple distraction can lead to the user paying a premium.

Even if the expression dark pattern does not have a legislative definition, the problems raised by these techniques for creating digital interfaces are attracting the attention of jurists in various liberal systems, who recognize forms of abuse of contractual freedom in them.[42]

In particular, we can note that, both in the context of the US and the European legal systems, we are becoming aware of the problems associated with these practices.[43]

Furthermore, due to the lack of a shared terminology among legal practitioners, US jurists have only recently been able to frame numerous actions of the Federal Trade Commission (FTC), which combats dark patterns without naming them.[44]

---

[39] Luguri and Strahilevitz (2021).

[40] Mathur et al. (2019).

[41] Deceptive Design - user interfaces crafted to trick you. https://www.deceptive.design/. Accessed 25 October 2022.

[42] In fact, the practices that fall under the category of dark patterns appear to reflect all the constitutive elements of the abuse of the right, as they result from an analysis of juridical and doctrinal uses. Also see Giorgio Pino (2006).

[43] Luguri and Strahilevitz (2021).

[44] Ibid., p. 84.

Again within the context of the US legal system, the Consumer Financial Protection Bureau (CFPB)[45] has adopted an extremely broad definition of abusive conduct, such as the inclusion of dark patterns. An abusive practice, according to 12 U.S.C. § 5531, is a practice that:

(1) Materially interferes with a consumer's ability to understand a term or condition of a financial product or service; or
(2) takes unreasonable advantage of
   (i) a lack of understanding of the material risks, costs, or conditions of the product or service on the part of the consumer;
   (ii) the consumers' inability to protect their interests when choosing or using a financial product or service; or
   (iii) the consumers' reasonable reliance on a person who should act in their (the consumers') best interests.

This provision would apparently cover the exploitation of consumers' cognitive biases in order to manipulate them into making a decision that may not be in their best interests.[46]

The Bureau européen des unions de consommateurs (BEUC) recently published a recommendation addressed to the European legislator concerning dark patterns[47] in which it highlighted the relevance of the Unfair Commercial Practices Directive (UCPD)[48] for regulating dark patterns. The directive (Article 5) refers to the concepts of "honest market practice," "good faith," and "good market practice;" according to the BEUC, this means that

> [t]raders must prevent consumers from being misled or influenced by a user interface guiding them to take a certain decision without having the possibility to understand the consequences of such a decision.[49]

Article 9 of the same directive prohibits traders from imposing any non-contractual obstacle if a consumer intends to exercise contractual rights, including the right to terminate a contract, return a purchase, or choose another supplier.

In addition to the UCPD, the BEUC deems the Unfair Contract Terms Directive (UCTD) to be relevant for the regulation of the use of interactive interfaces in commercial practices;[50] in particular, Article 5 requires terms that are not negotiated individually to be provided "in plain and understandable language." In the guidance document of the directive, the Commission indicated that, when assessing

---

[45] The Consumer Financial Protection Bureau (CFPB) is a US government agency that is responsible for consumer protection in the financial sector.

[46] Luguri and Strahilevitz (2021), p. 91.

[47] BEUC (2020) 'Dark patterns' and the EU consumer law acquis. https://www.beuc.eu/position-papers/dark-patterns-and-eu-consumer-law-acquis. Accessed 6 September 2022.

[48] Directive 2005/29/EC.

[49] BEUC (2020) 'Dark patterns' and the EU consumer law acquis. https://www.beuc.eu/position-papers/dark-patterns-and-eu-consumer-law-acquis. Accessed 6 September 2022, p. 6.

[50] Council Directive 93/13/EEC.

compliance with this requirement, it is necessary to consider the "way in which the contractual conditions are presented," including aspects such as "the clarity of the visual presentation, including the size of the characters, the presence of a logical structure and the highlighting of important clauses, which must have the necessary prominence and must not be hidden among other provisions." This interpretation makes the UCTD a relevant tool for ensuring that the contractors are not abusing the contractual freedom through the dark patterns and, in particular, the freedom of form by preventing the user from making a conscious and informed negotiation choice.

The European legislator has recently turned its attention to the problems associated with the misleading use of semiotic tools in the design of digital platforms. There was a major development in the area of internet platform legislation on 20 January 2022 as a result of the European Commission's approval of the final amendments to the Digital Services Act (DSA) that explicitly mentions dark patterns (recital 67).[51] This, in conjunction with the proposed Digital Markets Act (DMA), constitutes some of the most significant reforms in internet platform legislation in recent history.

6.5 Conclusion

Intersemiotic legal translation in the digital environment can increase the effectiveness of the legal act and make it more dynamic. However, this phenomenon can be considered to be a form of resemiotization (Sect. 5.2.3), which could sometimes be problematic.[52]

The smart contract code appears to be a clear example of resemiotization. In fact, unlike contractual clauses, it provides for automatic fulfillment based on the occurrence of specific conditions. In other words, unlike traditional contracts, smart contracts cannot be subject to non-fulfillment.

In summary, intersemiotic translation can be part of the process leading to the production of digital legal acts.

Intersemiotic translation can make legal content more accessible, even to non-specialized users.

From a legal point of view, resemiotization could be a problematic aspect of intersemiotic legal translation because it could lead to a target text that is different in kind from the source text. In other words, resemiotization could lead to a state of affairs that are in conflict with the user's original legal intent.

While the intent connected to the use of intersemiotic translation techniques in contract drafting and digital contract drafting, supported by legal design theorists, is explicitly aimed at facilitating the understanding of the contractual content, some techniques could be a source of misunderstanding on the part of the signatory

[51] The Regulation (EU) 2022/2065 will apply from 17 February 2024.

[52] Iedema (2003), p. 41.

contractor who has not drawn up the contract, which could lead to unforeseen and disadvantageous consequences.

The use of inadequate semiotic tools in the drafting of contracts could be understood as a form of abuse of contractual freedom. In fact, while the free choice of semiotic tools normally falls within the rights of the contractor who draws up the contract (unless otherwise provided by law), this could make it extremely difficult (if not impossible) for the other party in some cases. The contractor must be adequately informed about the content of the agreement. More precisely, the exercise of contractual freedom and freedom of form can be understood as abusive when it is in conflict with the right of the contractor to receive adequate information about the content of the agreement; that is, information that is clear, complete, truthful, faithful, unambiguous, and not deceptive.[53]

References

Addis A, Loddo OG, Saba M (2021) Social acts in digital environments. Phenomenology and Mind 20: 64-75. https://doi.org/10.17454/pam-2006

Amare N, Manning A (2013) A unified theory of information design: visuals, text and ethics. Routledge, London

Austin JL (1953) How to talk—some simple ways. Proceedings of the Aristotelian Society 53:227–246

Blount S (2015) Electronic contracts, 2nd edn. LexisNexis Butterworths, Australia

Boehme-Neßler V (2011) Pictorial Law. Modern law and the power of pictures. Springer, Berlin

Brownsword R (2019) Law, technology and society: re-imagining the regulatory environment. Routledge, Abingdon

Brownsword R (2021) Law 3.0. Routledge, New York

Burton SJ (2009) Elements of contract interpretation. Oxford University Press, Oxford

Cervone L, Palmirani M, Vitali F (2020) The intelligible contract. In: Proceedings of the 53rd Hawaii International Conference on System Sciences, pp 1780–1789

Corrales Compagnucci M, Haapio H, Fenwick M (2022) The many layers and dimensions of contract design. In: Compagnucci Corrales M, Haapio H (eds) Research handbook on contract design. Elgar, Cheltenham

Corrales M, Fenwick M, Haapio H (eds) (2019) Legal tech, smart contracts, and blockchain. Springer, Singapore

Cuccuru P (2017) Beyond bitcoin: an early overview on smart contracts. International Journal of Law and Information Technology 25:179–195. https://doi.org/10.1093/ijlit/eax003

Giancaspro M (2017) Is a 'smart contract' really a smart idea? Insights from a legal perspective. Computer Law and Security Review 33:825–835. https://doi.org/10.1016/j.clsr.2017.05.007

Glatt C (1998) Comparative issues in the formation of electronic contracts. International Journal of Law and Information Technology 6:34–68

[53] In this sense, § 307 abs seems interesting. 1 of the BGB. (Translation and italics are mine)

(1) The clauses in the general terms and conditions are ineffective if they result in an unreasonable disadvantage to the contractual partner contrary to the requirements of good faith. *An unreasonable disadvantage may also arise from the fact that the provision is not clear and understandable.*

Governatori G, Idelberger F, Milosevic Z et al (2018) On legal contracts, imperative and declarative smart contracts, and blockchain systems. Artif Intell Law 26:377–409. https://doi.org/10.1007/s10506-018-9223-3

Iedema R (2003) Multimodality, resemiotization: extending the analysis of discourse as multi-semiotic practice. Visual communation 2:29–57. https://doi.org/10.1177/1470357203002001751

Lamela Seijas P, Thompson S (2018) Marlowe: financial contracts on blockchain. In: Margaria T, Steffen B (eds) Leveraging applications of formal methods, verification and validation. Industrial practice. Springer International Publishing, Cham, pp 356–375

Loddo OG, Addis A, Lorini G (2022) Intersemiotic translation of contracts into digital environments. Frontiers in Artificial Intelligence 5: 1–16

Lorini G, Moroni S (2020) How to make norms with drawings: an investigation of normativity beyond the realm of words. Semiotica 2020:55–76. https://doi.org/10.1515/sem-2018-0062

Lorini G, Moroni S (2022) Non-Propositional Regulation. Philosophical Investigations 45:512–527. https://doi.org/10.1111/phin.12343

Luguri J, Strahilevitz LJ (2021) Shining a light on dark patterns. Journal of Legal Analysis 13:43–109. https://doi.org/10.1093/jla/laaa006

Marzotto G (2008) Il contratto point and click: il problema dell'autonomia negoziale. In: Moro P (ed) Etica informatica e diritto. FrancoAngeli, Milano, pp 222–250

Mathur A, Acar G, Friedman MJ et al (2019) Dark patterns at scale: findings from a crawl of 11K shopping websites.Proceedings of the ACM on Human-Computer Interaction 3:1–32. https://doi.org/10.1145/3359183

Sykora M (2017) Web 1.0 to Web 2.0: an observational study and empirical evidence for the historical r(evolution) of the social web. IJWET 12:70. https://doi.org/10.1504/IJWET.2017.084024

Olivecrona K (1971) Law as fact, 2nd edn. Stevens & Sons, London

Pino G (2006) L'abuso del diritto tra teoria e dogmatica (precauzioni per l'uso). In: Maniaci G (ed) Eguaglianza, ragionevolezza e logica giuridica. Giuffrè, Milano, pp 115–175

Plaza J (1987) Tradução intersemiótica. Perspectiva, São Paulo

Searle JR (1969) Speech acts: an essay in the philosophy of language. Cambridge University Press, Cambridge

Searle JR (1989) How performatives work. Linguistics and Philosophy 12:535–558

Smith B (2014) Document acts. In: Konzelmann-Ziv A, Schmid HB (eds) Institutions, emotions, and group agents: contributions to social ontology. Springer, Dordrecht, pp 19–31

Stazi A (2021) Contract and technology from automatic to telematic contracts. In: Stazi A (ed) Smart contracts and comparative law: a Western perspective. Springer, Cham, pp 3–28

Szabo N (1997) Formalizing and Securing Relationships on Public Networks. First Monday 9 https://doi.org/10.5210/fm.v2i9.548

Chapter 7
Conclusions

The use of non-linguistic semiotic systems in legal communication is increasing. The use of icons, diagrams, and even comic strips and illustrations is becoming more common in legal documents, such as contracts or privacy policies, to communicate legislative innovations and to indicate the key features of current legislation.

However, lawyers have mainly focused on the linguistic dimension of legal communication, and have omitted the intersemiotic dimension. Due to education and practice, lawyers and courts are affected by a logocentric prejudice. There are no corresponding traditions in law to guide the interpretation of other semiotic tools.

We have attempted to demonstrate that the semiotic tools that are available to contemporary jurists are manifold. Due to the advancement of information technology and digital law, intersemiotic translations will gain ever-increasing importance in the legal profession.

The aim of this book is not to cultivate an idealized view of the current situation; the aim of this research is to provide an overview, albeit partial, of the forms of intersemiotic legal translation that are currently in use by taking their limitations, possible distortions, and potential into account.

Signs are simply tools; like any tool, they can be used to produce positive outcomes such as reducing language barriers, making legal instruments more accessible for the common person, promoting social inclusion, simplifying economic exchanges and legal interactions, and preventing conflicts and lawsuits. However, the application of the techniques of intersemiotic translation can also be used ideologically to communicate the content of unjust laws, to deceive a contractor, to take advantage of the cognitive biases of a user, or otherwise provide an unfair advantage over others.

Nonetheless, these tools are part of a cultural and legal vista with which contemporary lawyers are already grappling.

Therefore, lawyers and legal scholars can no longer afford to ignore the limitations or the potential of intersemiotic legal translation.

O. G. Loddo, *Intersemiotic Legal Translation*, Law and Visual Jurisprudence 11,
https://doi.org/10.1007/978-3-031-44184-4_7